THE LOVE FIELD

*A Spiritual Therapy Guide
To Help You Heal and Liberate
Yourself From Psychic Pain, Emotional
Dependency, And Fearful Living*

ELENA MORARU

THE LOVE FIELD:
A Spiritual Therapy Guide To Help You Heal and Liberate
Yourself From Psychic Pain, Emotional Dependency,
And Fearful Living

ISBN: 979-8-9857728-0-7 (Paperback Edition)
ISBN: 979-8-9857728-1-4 (eBook Edition)

Library of Congress Catalog Card Number: 2022902994

To my daughter, whose existence has birthed the woman through which this book could come through.

CONTENTS

INTRODUCTION

*O*ne day in March of 2021, I was seated in a meditation course taught by Michael Bernard Beckwith. This session had started with the words:

"Imagine yourself stepping into a LOVE FIELD, where you feel completely accepted, nourished, loved, and nurtured. Think about a time when someone really understood you and loved you and expand that feeling into this moment."

I was frozen for several seconds in one of those moments where time slows down because I realized that I had never had a moment in my life where I felt this way. The closest moment I could picture was one spent in the presence of my mother, but even that moment felt conditioned in some way, as though I had to be someone or do something in order to be worthy of her attention and love.

I had a good childhood. There was not a lot of drama compared to other people's lives, and my parents loved us in their own way. I was born in a post-Soviet country where people didn't really know that terms like "happy" or "love" in our vocabulary *actually existed*. My parents did love my siblings and me, but they did not feel comfortable with really sharing it with us. It just wasn't part of our culture, so as a result, we grew up not truly knowing for sure if we were

being loved and accepted just the way we are. Thus, unconditional love sounded foreign to me, as it does for many of
others today.

I instantly associated the concept of this Love Field
with a power I had no idea existed or felt before; I had been
rationalizing the existence of God. But in that moment, for
the first time, I could consciously articulate what the nature
of my Heavenly Father felt like.

I was raised in a family that was considered Christian Orthodox but attended church only on Easter. However, thanks
to my grandmother, I have been aquatinted with Christ from
when I was a young girl. This being said, I do not consider myself religious or connected to any particular dogma. I consider
that the Truth of the Most High is being expressed through
many texts and languages, but the message is always the same.
I do not proclaim that this book contains the absolute truth.

Back to the concept of the Love Field, it is one thing to
express it in words, but it is another thing to truly experience
it. The thing is, this Love Field exists. It is a place not inside
or outside of us; it is a place where we all concomitantly exist.
This place feels so strange for us because we've been raised to
think and feel very conditionally towards ourselves, people,
and the environment around us. In this Love Field—and
I call it like that because that is exactly what it is—you see
things without attachment, you feel completely safe and
protected, light, and incredibly loved by something that is
present in you, above you, around you, and below you.

I decided to write this book because I believe that this
Love Field is what we are all searching for; it is the destination we all crave, and fortunately it exists in the blink of an

eye within our consciousness. This is a place where everything and everyone is free, where there are no judgments, no contradictions, and only peace, joy, and freedom. What a wonderful realization it is to know that we do not have to work to enter the Love Field, we do not have to impress God to have access to it, we do not have to meditate for hours or years, we do not have to be something or do something. We simply have to hold the desire in our heart to be in the Love Field and instantly we can be there. It is available and it is part of God's Kingdom for us. I even feel this could be the Kingdom Itself.

The Love Field is not a place, not even a destination; it is a reality. A *Course in Miracles* states that beneath our thoughts and words is written the Word of God. A way to find out the Word of God is to first realize that everything we consciously see and think is not real; reality is not in separation, in jealousy, in anger, in division. Nothing of that nature really exists—only love is real. At the beginning of studying *A Course in Miracles*, I had a tough time understanding these ideas, but after experiencing the Love Field, I have come to understand what this really means.

You might wonder at this point: "Well, Elena, all you say is really great, but life is full of struggles, pain, and suffering. We can't just ignore or deny that." I understand why you would think this, and I want to disclose that I also thought the same thing until recent years of experiencing the Love Field.

Here's my example of how reality can look different than what is seen. After the global pandemic hit, I stopped watching the news . I still do not watch absolutely anything on television or the internet pertaining to the news, and I even gave up my personal social media accounts, which gave me news whether I wanted it or not. If I need information, I just open Google and find out immediately if there is something that needs my attention.

The reason I am sharing this is because people would call me from other parts of the world and ask me, "How is life in Texas?" And I would reply, "Oh, everything is great, life is going well." Then they would respond, "That's strange because what it shows on TV is very different than what you say." And I told them to stop watching the news because reality is very different than what's on the screen, particularly my reality because I decide what to see and what to make space for in my life.

It is the same thing with life's struggles, pain, and suffering. No one says to deny the existence of these states of being or experiences of others. But ultimately, it is your decision what to see. Pain and suffering have a very high spiritual purpose. They do not last a long time if you learn what needs to be learned and move on. As for my own life, I think it's because of my pain and suffering that I have come to understand that nothing, absolutely nothing, can bring me complete freedom, fulfillment, unconditional love, and peace except my relationship with God.

Reality is what we individually make of it. We have been given absolute freedom to choose in this life. This is a task hard to grasp at first, but I will guide you through this book on how to access the Love Field. And once you do, your life will never be the same. You will stand and breathe in the Divine Presence of the Christ within you while your Creator fills you with His absolute love and adoration for you.

PART I

THEORY

CHAPTER 1

INTENTION

"Every action, thought, and feeling is motivated by an intention, and that intention is a cause that exists as one with an effect. If we participate in the cause, it is not possible for us not to participate in the effect."
– Gary Zukav

I have contemplated very often in my life what the word love really and truly means. We are so accustomed to so many definitions and experiences of love. Love has been defined in the dictionary this way:

Love: an intense feeling of deep affection.

Then I got curious about how affection is defined:

Affection: a gentle feeling of fondness or liking.

It felt like the dictionary was seriously playing with me, so I looked up what fondness is:

Fondness: affection or liking for someone or something

The bottom line is that love is defined by the dictionary as a feeling you have when you like someone or something. Many of us agree with this definition; we often use the word love when we *like* something. But the truth is that to love is very different than to like—no matter if it pertains to people, things, Earth, or even God. I have come to understand that when we are in the presence of this beautiful feeling, in a situation when this is directed to someone, there are different words that articulate it, such as these:

I hear you. I see you. I am here for you. I honor you.

The mistake we are making is loving people we like, or we think we like, and then attributing to them the label of someone we love, which keeps us from experiencing the true nature of love. The same thing happens with ourselves. Many times, when we decide to turn towards ourselves and cultivate a loving attitude, we think we need to consciously start liking who we are and what we do, counting and looking for things our mind might agree is okay, beautiful, and right about us. Here, again, we have the wrong approach!

Loving ourselves is not rooted in liking ourselves, and that is because our mind likes things. So liking is very entangled with a rational understanding of things, but love, love is the original cause from where thoughts can originate. Love is the first cause. This is the reason why love is different from like.

Love does not originate in the mind from a physical plane. First, it can be felt in your body. After that, it can reach the mind. Love is a very high vibrational energy; it might even be the highest. The way that everything heals, dissolves, and is enriched with joy, peace, and abundant life energy in the presence of love shows us what a powerful energy love truly is. Love is an essential requirement for us to be able to access and embody God as often as possible.

At this point, here is what is important to understand and remember: love is not a rational understanding in our consciousness, but a state of being where you embody the most powerful force of the Universe.

Oftentimes, when I sat in guided meditations, I noticed the guide almost always had to direct the meditator to imagine

6

a situation or person outside of yourself to bring them to a state of being where they could feel gratitude, appreciation, and love. But I've thought a lot about this over time. It's very imprisoning to believe in the idea that someone or something, such as a memory, can bring into you elevated states of being. The truth is that we imprison ourselves because of a lack of understanding ourselves and understanding God. We can look within ourselves to find love.

There are depths in our being that are extremely unexplored. And when I say extremely unexplored, I mean that many of us live our days going about life with no consideration of what's inside the human being we see reflected in the mirror, even if we meditate daily or go to church.

Marianne Williamson has said that our deepest fear is not that we are inadequate, our deepest fear is that we are powerful beyond measure. Intellectually this statement does not enter our subconscious mind easily, since we live in a society and a world where a single person is not seen as significant or important. A lot of us would say, "Well, there are almost 8 billion of us and if everyone would be important and significant, it would be an impossible world."

The truth is that we are all important and significant, but we just do not look properly at ourselves. And this is the reason for the confusion that exists. We look only with our physical eyes, and we see only a gathering of bones. What a tragedy it is to have this type of narrow vision for just a brief second when we could be seeing things through the eyes of love, yet it's the vision most of us live with daily.

Finding Love Within Exercise

Stand in front a mirror and look into your eyes for at least two whole minutes. Look deeply, beyond the physical body, beyond the personality. Look beyond everything you know, or think you know, about yourself. And after that, look even more deeply than you think you can. Stay open to what you feel as you do this.

I guarantee you will be surprised by what you see.

In religious and spiritual texts, it's common to hear people talk about our magnificence, but it's often spoken about without context. We are left without a proper understanding of the nature of this magnificence, where it comes from, and how to handle it. The understanding of this magnificence is especially misguided when in our day there is the self-help industry, where every person tries to sell you the idea that you are great. "So let's explore this greatness of yourself and get you going," self-help guides will try to convince you. Seriously, it is hard not to become sick of this perception of magnificence and just ignore the idea altogether.

Our nature originates in the essence of Universal Divine energy, of God, of your Heavenly Father, or whatever name you have for your Creator. If we look only at our bodies, because that is what the physical eyes can see first, we'd notice our bodies are a magnificent creation. We as individuals by ourselves (i.e., with the power of our ego) could not in a million years or more bring forth such a brilliant thing as the human body. Not to mention the life force, guidance, intuition, energy, the flowing power that resides and moves through us, which cannot be perceived with our physical eyes, but that

8

we can only physically witness the presence of it through the results of its existence and movement in our lives. That is something we could never create on our own; only God, our Creator, could have done this. Only ignorance keeps us away from a true vision of who we are: creations of God.

As I mentioned, I reflected for some time on the fact that I was unable to picture a moment of feeling unconditional love in my life. I also realized that by being unable to discern such an experience for myself, I probably have not been able to extend it to others. Or to put this into simpler words, I haven't been able to make others feel unconditionally accepted, supported, and loved: be that my child, partner, mother, or other close people that I think I *love.*

I realized to extend love to others, I needed to be filled with it. And first I needed to extend it to myself because I knew that only when you feel totally accepted, loved, and supported can you give this experience to others. Yet my conscious self debated the idea by saying, "Well, if it is me, then how do I activate it or make it rise and exist?"

The answer to this question is that I cannot. I, by myself cannot *think* myself into growing love inside myself, no matter how many hours of meditations I go through. This can only happen by surrendering to who I am. Surrendering to who I am means that I open my consciousness, my heart, and my mind to the presence of the One who knows how to do it—I let God rise where He already abides. I surrender to the Greatest Power in the universe, allowing Him to flow through me, to show me who I am, to reveal Himself through my mind and my heart, and to bring forth the truth of the immense and unmeasurable love that He has for me.

9

We are always in communion with God, it's just that we have deviated so much in our consciousness from this truth that we need to bring ourselves back to the realization of our Oneness with our Creator. It is God who gives you the realization that you are completely loved, accepted, and supported. But even though God brings you the experience, you need to allow it; you need to open yourself to it.

We've been created free. An energy like love cannot live and exist in restricted environments or conditions, so we had to be created with free will for it to exist in ourselves. The concept of free will is also the reason why lots of misconceptions about God and life exist today.

Growing up as a Christian Orthodox, I was introduced to Christ and the divine nature of life, which I am very thankful for. But my religious experience also caused me to fear God, to believe that I was not of God, and that I am a sinner. The teachings told me that we are imperfect children who need to ask for forgiveness or otherwise their judgmental Father will punish them for their sins. And one of the worst punishments is burning for an eternity in a very bad place.

I have attended various Orthodox churches in different parts of the world throughout my life while searching for true communion with God. Part of me would be completely at ease while attending services until I opened one of the books sitting next to the Bible in the chair's pocket, a particular book where a set of church rules would be listed. One of them was, and it was written something like this: "We are people with fear of God and if attending this church, it is required that you be respectful and on time for service. It is unacceptable for anyone to be late and disturb services, but if you do come late, please wait so that a member of staff can seat you at the right time."

First, I thought the people that wrote these rules for sure have no children of their own. Second, I thought, "So everyone coming here needs to understand they need to be afraid of God?" I began to notice that many religions promoted this fear of God.

One thing for all of us to understand is that you cannot love what you are afraid of; you cannot be open to someone or to something of which you are afraid. Fear and love are two opposite realities. You either feel fear or feel love—both at the same time cannot exist.

A response concerning the fear of God that I always get from my fellow Christian Orthodox community, and others as well, is this: "Elena, if people do not fear God, then they would be going around hurting everyone and doing whatever they want only for their own selfish reasons." Yet people don't do bad things and hurt others because they're not afraid of God, the truth is they do it because they think they are separate from others and from God.

Only when someone thinks, "You are there and I am here, and whatever happens to you does not affect me in any way," can someone do things that might harm others. This is because, based on this illusionary vision of separation, people who harm others believe they are not harmed in any way by these actions. This is the biggest lie and problem of our existence.

A Course in Miracles says, "There is no place that I end, and you begin." We are all united in one mind, in one energy, and in one consciousness. If someone's hurting, it

11

affects us all. We might not be consciously aware of it, but it does. You can continue to believe in your separation, but reality slams you every day with the truth that I am you and you are me. At the deepest core of who we are, we actually love and care about each other because that is the nature of our magnificence, that is the nature of God.

To enter the Love Field, first you need to open to God so that He can take up the space in our hearts and our consciousness. Only God's presence can teach you unconditional love because this is the place where it originates. Once you communion with the Divine, you learn how to carry this vibrational frequency with you everywhere you go and step back into it when you slip away.

After you learn this, you can begin to extend this unconditional love towards yourself since God has already done that and taught you how to do it too. At this point, only after you have opened to this unconditional love within yourself, you can begin to extend to give it to others. It's important to remember that you do not get into relationships with other people to get the energy of love, but to bring this energy with you.

Now you're ready to enter the Love Field. This book will guide you through different steps and approaches that you can take to wake up and heal yourself from the illusion of separation. Once you experience your communion with God, it is almost impossible to go back to being your old ego-governed self because you can see and feel clearly Who has always abided within you.

To experience something, it's helpful to set an intention. Intention is what produces the outcome. I believe we create our reality through the power of our intention. In my own life, I have noticed that everything that happens has an existing intention, whether I am aware of it or not. Creating an intention is a good starting point for the life-changing experience of entering the Love Field because it will help to keep you focused during your spiritual transformation.

To access the Love Field, we need to set up the intention to get there, but also stay open to how that will unfold particularly for you. You can use the information in this chapter to set up your intention to access that place of unconditional love within you.

CHAPTER 2

PRESENT MOMENT

"Remember the breath. It's a talisman for the present moment that leads you into the eternal now."
– Michael Bernard Beckwith

$\mathcal{E}$ very experience that we go through is always happening right now. Everything that we went through previously or think we will go through in the future does not actually exist in the present moment, even if we try and articulate these experiences. The understanding of reality requires a clear understanding of time. Time is not something that exists; it is an illusion of the mind. Memory is what creates time.

Everything that we are and have been through exists right here and right now; everything we think we want in the future exists right now. Doctor Joe Dispenza discusses time in his books. In his last book *Supernatural*, he gives explicit facts based on quantum theories about time. Quantum physics is the study of matter and energy at its most fundamental level. Based on quantum theory, everything that exists, exists right now in this moment.

The fact that you want something that you think you do not have means it already exists but at a different level of vibration in another dimension. You still do not have it because you are not a vibrational match to that which you want. This idea about reality and time brings us to the fact that the present moment is an important factor to consider in perceiving reality.

We all have had moments when we felt we have lost track of time. This is actually a moment of transcendence, with life flowing through the present moment. This is exactly how life is meant to be: completely present to what is happening in front of us in each moment. Only by being present to this degree can we understand life and reality truthfully.

What usually goes on in our heads at any given moment is mostly the activity of a big pile of memories trying to create a certain understanding of what is currently happening in our lives. When we make the effort to become more present and build the habit, we get to witness an encounter with a raw vision on life, our true selves, and God. Life, our soul, and God can only be revealed in the present moment. This present moment is a very sacred space because it's the prerequisite for our most profound experience. The question now is how do you develop a habit of tuning in to the present moment, or how do we transcend time?

First, we need to stop multitasking. No matter how busy we think our lives are and how trapped we are in the lives that we created; it is pivotal to stop creating this mental busyness. This only creates a chaotic inner world. We always have the choice, no matter the circumstances.

I will give you an example. After I became a mother, my relationship with life changed drastically. I had a constant deficit of time in my life. I felt my daughter came into this world to take over my life and leave me completely depleted of time spent with myself, which I basically worshiped before being a mom. What she actually taught me is that I am completely responsible for my own time, for my own choices, and no one has any authority in my life besides me.

Becoming a mother also taught me how to better understand the consequences of my decisions and to stop when I feel my cup is full. In the case of having children, for me, it meant I need to stop birthing human beings because I barely can handle taking care of me and her at the same time, so anyone else added to the circle would mean we would have a very difficult life. I think it is crucial to understand what you can handle in life and not overfill yourself to the point where you want to borrow a spaceship and leave the Earth. As a mother, I tell you, it is possible to bring peace to your mind and stop multitasking.

The second thing we can do to tune in to the present moment is to learn how to surrender and forgive. If you cannot surrender and forgive, your connection to the present moment is seldom going to happen because life is not all butterflies and roses. To connect with God, you need to learn to forgive and surrender the unpleasant moments, people, and circumstances of your life.

Jesus said that forgiveness is a way of life. Without forgiveness, we cannot see what is truthfully here. For this step, you also need to be able to open up and be humble. Only the Divine energy within you can help you forgive. We will delve deeper into the subject of forgiveness in the next chapter.

The third thing you can do to connect to the present moment is allow Something greater to guide you. If you do not have a spiritual practice, you can start with meditation and then move slowly to prayer (I guide you through both practices in the second part of the book). When we allow Something greater than us to step in to help us see things differently, we must make space in our consciousness for it. First, you recognize that the current rational activity of your brain cannot guide you because you are filled with memories of the past and plans of the future. Then when you allow Something greater to guide you, a very powerful thing happens—something inside you moves and awakens.

Everyone calls this force something different, but the best word for it is Energy because you can feel the flow of it moving through you. You become aware of this Energy, even when you thought that such a thing never existed, and it starts to fill you up in every moment that you pay attention and surrender to it. This Energy will guide you to see the present moment.

The metaphysical text, *A Course in Miracles* teaches that the way we see the world most of the time is not in our highest, best interest, because we do not see the truth. Yet the reality of things (the truth) beyond the veil of illusion is actually created for our highest, best interest.

When I first read this lesson in the course, I was thinking, "How on earth when someone dear to us suffers can it be in our highest best interest?!"

I've come to realize that we do not understand our hardships, and those of the people we love, because we have a very limited view on life.

This is the reason that tuning in to the present moment is important. When we are fully emerged in the here and now, we are more likely to see through the veil; we can consciously see a different world and look upon ourselves with different eyes. In the present moment, the thoughts of the past and of the future subside. According to science, when you are focused in the present moment, there is little mental activity in the prefrontal cortex (the most evolved part of your brain that does all the conscious thinking) and what is left is only presence. You become fully present to what is actually here in front of your eyes.

In this presence, you realize that you are not the one who is thinking. Rather, you are the one who is observing. And in this observation, you find deep peace and reverence for life, for what is inside you, and for God. The world and life are a wonderful place, if only we could tune in to it more deeply to see what magnificence is in and around us all. This can all happen in the present moment.

The Love Field, a place of unconditional love, can be seen, felt, and experienced only by being fully aware in the present moment. You cannot think yourself into it or plan your consciousness to get there. You can set an intention, but after that you need to allow what is inside you to take you there and fill you with love. You cannot grasp, you can only allow it. If you try and grasp it, it dissipates, but if you allow it, it will fill you and it will be everywhere.

I personally consider the present moment to also be a very powerful healing instrument. If you have any physical ailment or a mental, emotional, or spiritual problem, connecting to the present moment usually lifts a lot of the burdens, stress, and mental pressure that is causing the problem. This is why people that meditate, pray, have a spiritual practice, and know how to sit in silence have better physical, emotional, and spiritual health.

The present moment is the only place where we can feel and understand God, Universal Divine Energy, and Spirit. I consider our bodies to be vehicles of our Divine Energy. We get stuck in life because we forget who we are. We look in the mirror and become so overwhelmed by thinking we are only a body—but what moves the body? What pumps that heart of yours? Where is that energy coming from? When we become more aware of where we are and how we feel, we can observe how the Energy inside us is being revealed. In the present moment we stop seeing with our physical eyes, and we start seeing with our Energy field. Some might say we start feeling everything around us, but what is actually happening is that true vision is embodying us.

The Love Field is where God fills you because only His Divine Energy can do that. No person, no thing, no other type of element with energetic charge can encompass you. We are divinely created and always protected. We suffer not because negative emotions fill us, but because our vision is being distorted. We do not see clearly.

We are always filled with God; we are just not always aware of this when we are in pain. Pain is not caused by something being done to us; pain is caused by forgetting who we are. *A Course in Miracles* says that when true vision is restored, there is nothing to be feared because there is nothing to be lost—where love abides, fear dissipates.

Our goal is to focus our consciousness on what is real because what we focus on expands. In this expansion of the nature and energy of God inside us and around us, we can find freedom, liberation, and purpose.

****

CHAPTER 3

AWARENESS

"Like an astronaut, you're carrying your own atmosphere with you, the atmosphere of self-love, appreciation, kindness, and support.
– Michael Bernard Beckwith

*W*hen I first sat in Michael Beckwith's meditation class, where I encountered the Love Field for the first time, it felt so new and so raw that I couldn't really believe I hadn't experienced such a thing until now. I did the meditation many times afterwards, and it has never felt like the first time. This is because I am already familiar with it; I am already aware of it.

Awareness is what wakes us up. It is what makes our lives never the same again since you can't go back to being unaware. In the case of this field of unconditional love, I had lived my entire life thinking I felt, knew, and was giving love to others. The truth is that I wasn't. And even today, after encountering the Love Field, I still struggle with the illusion of separation and filling myself with who I truly am. One of the reasons I am writing this book is to focus my attention on uncovering what unconditional love is so that I can expand it in my own life and become more often my real self.

My path towards God started when I was a kid watching the movie *The Life of Jesus*. I felt so amazed at the nature of His personality. I thought about how of all the people I knew no one could ever be as close to Him in their human behavior. As a child, I remember I always made it a goal to be like Jesus. This is because I felt the power of His presence. I wondered what it would be like to be so magnificent through the way He made other people feel around Him.

I also wanted that for my life; I wanted to heal and make others feel good the way He did.

Well, later in my life, I did not end up mirroring the nature of Jesus. At the time, this was because I thought life got in the way. I first went to pursue a degree that was not meant for me and a second one after that, which it turns out was not meant for me either. Yet now I finally understand that they were both meant for me. This is because the path for me to understand who Jesus was and what Christ is required all these different roads for me to get here.

Only recently did I come to understand who Christ is and who the Son of God is. This changed my life in a very significant way. *A Course in Miracles* says that Jesus was a man that saw the face of Christ in all His brothers and remembered God, so He became identified with Christ—a man no longer, but at one with God. One of the first steps in understanding our true nature is to understand who Christ is. Christ is that part of us that sees God in everything. Christ is the part of us that gives up on separation. Christ is the part of us that honors the body as a temple for His nature to rest in. Christ is the vertical energy through which we are connected to God.

If you haven't been raised as a Christian, I am sure you have your own version of Christ. It is the same energy, the same identity; it is our Divine Nature. It is that power within you that helps you forgive. It is the voice in your heart that moves you in directions that feel peaceful and joyful.

Becoming aware of Christ is the first step into understanding the spiritual nature of our lives. We need to stop moving around on Earth unaware of ourselves; it is time to embrace our spirituality. It is time to live as spiritual beings having a spiritual life.

Spiritual modalities related to God, such as different therapies, healings, and science with a mystic element involved have to stop being so out of normality and only for religious or spiritual people. We are all spiritual, spiritual beings, with our souls rooted in the nature of God.

We will continue to have all sorts of struggles if we decide to not answer this spiritual calling. Every pain, every moment of uncertainty is a call to pay attention, to look at life differently, and to see who and what is truly here. We've lived distracted lives for so long. If it's not one trendy industry, it is a next new one. And if it's not going to space, it is the internet. All of these things are actually existing to help us see beyond the physical. Every branch of science reveals God, every microscope is a tool to see the grandiosity of our Universe.

Many times, it is only our perception that is a problem; we decide to see what our hand can touch and totally disregard Who moves the hand and Who feels the sensation. I think the purpose of our evolution is awareness, awareness of Who has been creating the dots and organizing them so we can connect them. What a relief it is to know that we are indeed taken care of. We do not have to try and invent an idea about the Universe, because it has already been created and arranged in our best interests. Our job is to become aware of Who is truly here.

The moment we embrace our Christ nature, we start choosing in every situation how to feel and what to do. The outcome is very different when our intention is to act from that place within where Christ resides. I believe for me, had I not been such a seeker of God, going into prayer and answering the call to get into prayer, I might have not experienced the Love Field yet. I believe that your seeking is what sets up the intention that can get you there. Though the Love Field is not a physical place; it is a level of your consciousness.

No matter what is going on in your life, you need to trust and understand that all is happening is for you to turn your attention to God, no matter what you believe in or if you consider yourself spiritual or not. The fact that you think you are not of God does not deny your True Nature. You are still the child of the Most High God.

It will take you some time to become aware of this, depending on how much you decide to explore the subject in your consciousness. I remember very well my moments of losing myself where I would say, "Well, it would be nice to pray and meditate and go to church and read about spirituality and God, but I have to make money. I have to take care of so many things and there is so much stress in my life that I cannot really do this right now."

Oh boy, how wrong I was! Now I can clearly see that even when you feel that life is withholding something from you, it does this so that you can put your time and attention on something else and stop grasping what you *think* is good for you. Many times what we think is good for us is not what the Divine thinks is good for us. Most of the time we need to trust and let the flow of everything take us where we need to go. There is a reason why we are in a particular place doing a particular thing.

Eventually, we do come to a place of peace, to a place of surrender, and if we continue to look for the real thing, it will get us to places we think are not of this world. And that happens because we are not of this world, we are of God.

That moment we decide to accept and embody our Divine Nature is when we can start welcoming in our lives emotions and feelings like self-love, kindness, appreciation, support, patience, and forgiveness. That happens because these are attributes of the nature of God. When we embrace God within ourselves, these characteristics of ourselves start blossoming because now we do not identify with scarcity, lack, limitation, and separation from God any longer.

It would be very hard to define God, but just a glimpse of what it is I think the Bible verses 1 Corinthians 13:4-8 tell us:

> *4 Love is patient and kind; love does not envy or boast; it is not arrogant 5 or rude. It does not insist on its own way; it is not irritable or resentful;[a] 6 it does not rejoice at wrongdoing, but rejoices with the truth. 7 Love bears all things, believes all things, hopes all things, endures all things. 8 Love never ends.*

Bears all things, believes all things, hopes all things, endures all things: love never ends. This is the nature of the Divine—eternal, limitless, all loving, all accepting, and all unconditionally.

With our human nature, there will be resistance in accepting mentally such concept. But because unconditional love, God, and the Divine is not something that is outside of ourselves but also what is inside of ourselves, we can overcome the resistance easily. The solution is to pay attention and connect daily; look for Christ in everything, in everyone. Make it a part of your vision, no matter what you are doing or have in front of you. Know that God is more powerful than your distorted vision that brings pain and suffering. Amid all the wrongs that are happening, you can ask for resurrection. You can ask for the Christ within to step into your consciousness and bring you the revelation that you are breathing, sitting in the most sacred space there is, and there is nothing to fear. You are already home; you are already safe.

A Course in Miracles says that if we would know who walks beside us at all times, fear would be impossible. It is only by allowing God to step into your perception that you can understand and feel that He has been and is with you at all times.

FORGIVENESS

In order to move past the limitations of your conscious mind and get to experience the nature of the Divine, a very important step is necessary. This is the process of forgiveness. Our human nature requires forgiveness to exist because only in the process of forgiveness can we make the first steps to remember God. Forgiveness is the greatest shift in energy, and it can bring freedom and purpose to your life.

Forgiveness brings God where there is no God. Forgiveness brings love where there was only fear and lack. Forgiveness transforms an entire reality, and shifts your perception from illusion to truth. Forgiveness reveals to you and those around you in any given situation the blissful nature of life. You can see peace where you could only see war; you can bring connection where there was only separation. With forgiveness, life flows through you with the guidance of the Divine. With forgiveness, you can know what true joy is. And only with forgiveness can you make room for love inside your heart. Jesus said that forgiveness is a way of life.

Here is how to forgive someone, something, yourself, or life circumstances:

1. You need to know that the Universe is for you and not against you; God is for you. Difficult life circumstances are not here for you to suffer or be in pain for any random reason. They are happening so you can transform into someone that God has created you to be. They are happening so you can overcome the veil, the veil of illusion, so you can see clearly what is true, what is important, and what matters while you are here on Earth. Everything you have endured or are currently going through is meant to bring you to a place closer to God, a place where you can rejoice in His presence and love. If someone has hurt you, it does not mean anything else besides the fact that you have given them a place in your life that does not belong to them, and you have given them a power that needed to stay only in your own hands. Only God is in a position to define who you are and what you are worth. And believe me, He thinks you are magnificent.

2. You open yourself up to God. Forgiveness is not a task of the ego. As your ego and your rationality cannot forgive. Forgiveness is a matter of the soul; only God helps you forgive. He has put inside you the technology to forgive. You surrender to Him and ask Him through meditation and prayer to step in and activate the faculty necessary inside your heart to forgive.

3. You sit with yourself and center yourself, taking deep breaths, walking in nature, sitting in silence, so you can clearly state your request to see things differently. And then you sit even more so you can hear and experience the shift in your perception about the person or circumstance that are the object of your asking.

4. You surrender to the present moment and accept the shift in energy. Sometimes the shift in energy might not happen right away, but you will slowly start to feel lighter, set free, and eventually liberated.

Forgiveness is a change in perspective that takes place at the soul level and then gets embodied in the conscious mind. It is a shift in energy. For forgiveness to happen, you need to become very humble and open to understanding life differently. In this life, there is usually nothing against us; we feel sometimes that there might be, but that is part of the illusion. Every person or situation reflects a state of being, and usually that state of being is our own because we mirror each other all the time. This state of being reveals itself this way, and then we question the goodness of that which is outside of us. But what is actually happening is that the voice of different parts of ourselves start to be loud so that we can pay attention to what is trying to be revealed or what needs transformation.

HYPNOTHERAPY

The reason I am bringing up hypnotherapy in this chapter is because I consider it a very powerful tool in cleaning yourself up so you can make space for God to rise within yourself. That's right, cleaning yourself up!

With hypnotherapy, you can access parts of your subconscious mind where a lot of your limited understanding of life and God has been stored. Many emotional and psychological traumas can be healed with hypnotherapy. Hypnotherapy is changing my life in an immensely powerful way at this very moment.

Also, the main principle to understand in any therapy is that it should be considered a tool that the Divine Energy uses to bring you to see the truth of who you are. The hypnotherapist I was going to had on one of her shelves a piece of art that said, "In this office, hypnotherapy is used as God's instrument for healing". Right in that moment, I knew I was in the right place.

With hypnotherapy, you can become aware of your True Nature because in hypnosis you can remember moments, such as when you were first conceived. I had a very amazing experience because I remembered who I was within my first hours of being in my mother's womb. I remember being so excited for this new path, and the other thing I remembered was that God was with me. There was this huge ball of light like a sun inside me. It was one of the most enlightening experiences I've had, feeling that lightness, sense of joy, and peace in me.

I know a lot of people are very skeptical towards hypnosis or other types of energy therapy. But I encourage everyone to at least try it and open yourself to it because energy or different levels of consciousness and awareness cannot enter where there is no door open; you will be pleasantly surprised by what you can discover.

In healing different parts of ourselves that were entangled in past experiences of our life, we release energy and make space inside ourselves for something else. Traumas and painful memories deeply stored in our subconscious build up in our consciousness, physical awareness, and mental activity. When you release them, it does not mean that you never remember them. It means your identity and your worth are not connected to them because you have untangled yourself and your idea of yourself from them. They just become events that happened in your life without any emotional or spiritual consequences on your consciousness.

This is the reason that I recommend hypnosis as a healing tool for your subconscious, for your consciousness, and your soul. After you clear a lot of stuff from your mind, you become aware of your soul. And when you become aware of your soul, a magnificent thing starts happening: the Universe expands in your consciousness and you become aware of God.

SILENCE AND SPACE

The Love Field, this space of unconditional love (I call it space because consciously it is easier to understand), is that place in your consciousness where you become aware of God. We understand Love, God, and any energy that exists within these fields differently compared with materiality. We cannot physically touch the energy, but we can see its effects. And one of the effects is the lightness, the peace, the joy in ourselves when we experience unconditional love.

For energy to be experienced in our consciousness, we need to make mental and energetic availability for it. That means training ourselves to sit in silence as much as possible because silence connects us to the present moment, which we discussed in Chapter 2. Silence is such a great conductor because our mind is constructed in such a way that can speed up in thinking, if we let it, to such a degree that it needs force to be stopped. That's why a person who never sits by themselves without any distraction finds it so difficult at first. They feel they must force themselves, that is the nature of mind; it feels like pushing forcefully on a brake in order to stop it. But as you sit more often in this silence, you will find yourself naturally drifting into a mental blank slate more easily.

In silence, everything subsides if you sit long and often enough. If you become a person who sits in silence a lot, you will notice many things. You will notice your thoughts and realize that what you mostly think about, yourself and everything else, is just thoughts. After some time, you train yourself to let go of everything, and that is when the magic starts happening.

35

As you let go, something else takes its space. And that something is your pure consciousness. Your pure consciousness is your True Nature. In your pure consciousness, you find God.

Your pure consciousness is not filled with anything; the Divine does not entitle itself as something, it just is. And you recognized it so well because you know it so well. You always did. And when you finally merge with it, you are home. It is the most incredible experience you will ever have because that is what you've always craved in your human understanding. You crave yourself because you are not yourself, and this is the reason you feel lost when you forget God.

EMPTINESS

Many times when I meditate and enter the Love Field, I find myself feeling that God is filling me. He is filling my soul, my mind, my body—every cell of my body. It is like a natural visualization of unifying with something so wonderful that the ease, the freedom, and the peace I feel are not of this world.

But one thing I started to realize is that this does not always happen, even if my intention is set up prior to that. Most often when unifying with the Love Field does not happen, it is because I am filled with stuff—with mental and emotional energy and imagery that is irrelevant to what I am trying to do. Actually, everything is irrelevant when you want to communion with God.

Many spiritual texts have talked about the idea that man, to be filled by God, first needs to empty himself and become nothing. This idea has nothing to do with the material world or what one egotistically possesses on this Earth. It has to do with who one is inside himself, with the ideas he has about himself and the world, with the sense of how he defines himself and everything that has happened, is happening, and thinks will happen to him.

The major purpose of hardships in our lives is to empty ourselves of preconceived ideas, dogmas, ways of thinking, and ways of perceiving things around us and in us. The purpose of the dark night of the soul is to purify the soul so God can enter. I want to make sure that we understand this correctly because I struggled to understand this at first. The dark night of the soul has the holy purpose it has for us.

I know people who even pray for the dark night of the soul, because the treasures it reveals are incredible. The treasures mean the clearing up of our vision to see the face and essence of God. Who wouldn't want that?

But many times, we stress more because something bad is happening to us than the actual stress being caused from the actual event. This is because we do not realize there is deeper purpose underneath it. And even if we cannot understand the dark night of the soul as its happening, after we come out on the other side, we can connect the dots and understand the necessity of that particular hardship in our lives.

Michael Beckwith said that pain pushes until vision pulls. When I first heard this, I had a huge "aha" moment. I realized how in my life I always tried to use introspection (vision) to grow and move forward in order to *avoid* pain. I always paid close attention to make sure I learned the lesson so that nothing bigger would come my way to wake me up. It worked many times, and it's still working because I set a goal to stay aware and listen when something is trying to teach me something.

But this does not mean I am able to completely avoid pain. I think that is quite impossible to do because to become aware, to grow, and to transform to be able to experience life in all its different dimensions, we need to move through change. And change is uncomfortable—so uncomfortable sometimes that it feels incredibly painful.

We all experience pain in our lives, no matter who we are in this world. The purpose of pain is to teach us and push us in directions necessary for the evolution of our soul. My most recent painful experience has cleared up a lot of illusion. I started my adult life interested in how to make a living, and this goal brought me to areas and industries that felt good at first. But then I started to feel lost again, without purpose. I realized that I needed to set up different goals: goals worthy of my soul. When we set goals worthy of our soul, the highest level of living becomes possible for us.

But it took quite a journey to come to this realization, and it still takes time to clear out part of the illusion that I learned throughout my childhood and teenage years. For some people, it takes a lot more time, years or even decades, and I think that's okay. There is always the energy of God moving us, no matter where we are in those moments of despair and moments of complete joy. We are never alone. It is important to understand and trust the process because the destination of any journey, of any path, is to bring us back to ourselves, to our True Nature, to the God within.

The question that can come up is, "If the soul needs to be purified through a dark night of the soul so God can fill it, does this mean that the soul is something different and separate from God?!" I assert separation from God is impossible, and the analogy is being wrongly understood. Our perception sees separation, but the soul is never separate from God—it is always filled with God. To put it in better words, during the dark night of the soul, our consciousness and our vision gets purified; we become aware of God and feel how the presence of Him envelops us when previously our vision was obscured. The filling-with-God process is actually a realization, which we will talk more about in a following chapter.

Recently, I was mentally very busy with to-do lists and things to accomplish, which we all are most of the time, but what I realized is that my lifestyle needed to be cleaner and less busy if I want to have space for God. I cannot handle mental clutter; I just don't function very well in this world without moments of silence and peace where I can enter emptiness, where all possibilities arise. I am not even interested in possibilities when I feel emptiness. I enjoy it so much that I couldn't care less about anything else that is happening because in emptiness I can feel God.

I know that to live in this world we need to-do lists; we need to go to work and to school; we need to cook and do and accomplish things. But it's important to understand what we need first. First we need to center ourselves, to feel the essence of our being, and to feel God. Only God can remind us to stay present and not lose ourselves in to-do lists and things that bring only temporary pleasures.

When we get centered and find God, we go into living our lives with more peace in our hearts, with more knowing that everything is okay, and we release the need to worry about the million things we have to do next. This is the reason that I think entering emptiness is important.

When we are emptied, we overcome our mind and our emotional baggage and triggers stored in our subconscious. In emptiness, we find freedom because it is the only place free of attachment, free of ideas, of resistance, of things to do or be. Emptiness is a prerequisite in finding and communing with God.

CHAPTER 4

REALIZATION

"There is no death because the Son of God is like his Father. Nothing you can do can change Eternal Love."
– A Course in Miracles

*R*ealization is the shift in consciousness—the change of vision that takes place when we experience the Divine in us. We realize there is nothing to grasp, to attach ourselves to, to hold on to because everything is already here; everything is already accomplished and done. In the realization of the Truth, the way many spiritual texts describe it, we find ourselves, our true selves, and we understand that there is no place to be, there is nowhere to go, because we are already where we need to be, and we are never away from our true selves.

True awareness is when one sees "I" in everything, when one sees God in themselves and everyone. When realization happens, it means that our life changes. It is impossible to get lost again in illusions of this world; we might get distracted for periods of time, but we can never forget.

When we see the face of God, we cannot be the same because the Truth is not something that you see and forget. The Truth has such a powerful impact on our consciousness that when we see It, we feel It. And we feel the Truth because we knew It all along. The Truth feels like home because It is home. Our true essence is our holiness, our God nature— where there is no sin and no illusion.

We have created an image of God through many religions and dogmas with our egotistic selves. Based on our egoic illusion, we created a God that punishes and is vengeful; a God that recognizes and believes in sin; a God whose creation is sinful. How can God's creation be sinful? His creation is like Himself, so there is no way that He could create us as sinners. We are created with love and filled with His love, enveloped and created with God's essence at our core.

Christ is not just Jesus; Christ is the Son of God in all of us. Realization in biblical terms means resurrection. Resurrection is the rise of Christ within us. Jesus demonstrated clearly who the Son of God is—He is the most Beloved Child of the Most Powerful Force in the Universe.

I use the word 'God' without constriction throughout this book and outside of it because I believe there is no better word. I don't think we should let religion or anything else obscure our relationship with the word. God is God, no matter what you call it. It is the Most High God, no matter what you believe in, your background, or if you like the word or not.

It is not the word that defines God; it is our consciousness that recognizes the power of God within the word. God is the greatest power in the Universe, and we should let nothing come in our way of recognizing this. I understand why some people are uncomfortable with the word 'God,' and I know that this is because of what I mentioned above about how some religions have defined and shared their vision of God. No wonder a lot of people grow not wanting to explore the spiritual nature of life and continue to live struggling, not finding peace through their life. Who would want to feel guilty and sinful all the time?

I just recently passed by a billboard where a church advertised itself by saying, "You need to recognize you are a sinner and accept Jesus into your life as your savior." There were some other requirements to be accepted by God and into the church too. I don't want to sound like I am against religions and churches. As I said before, thanks to Christian Orthodoxy, I have become familiar with Christ and with God. The problem is not in the *Bible*, the problem is in how the *Bible* and other spiritual texts have been translated and communicated. Religion has turned people away from God and towards illusions.

I hope this book brings you the Truth, which has been interpreted in many ways, and that what you get from reading this is that you are a miraculous creation of God, you are filled with God, and love is your only nature. You are not flawed; your vision is obscured. You are a beloved child of the Most High God. This is the only essence of who you are. From this core belief, you can sprout and let experiences unfold in your life that reveal the beauty—the extraordinary and the marvelous nature of our Creator. We are never separate. We are always connected because oneness is all there is.

Realization of the Truth liberates us because the illusions of this world imprison us, and there is no reason to argue this because we feel it every day. We feel discord when we are out of alignment with ourselves. We feel pain and suffering when we move away from God. And we feel free, connected, loved, and a deep sense of peace when we let ourselves be guided in the right direction—one that has communion with God as its goal.

I realized the goal of everything in life is communion with the Divine. Marriage, having a child, building a career, sustaining any relationship, everything—the purpose of everything is God. When we are not aware of it and think we're going to go ahead and marry and have a family because we don't want to be alone, or that everyone has one and it is the right thing to do, or whatever reason one has when going into any relationship—be that with people, work, or money—if the intentions and goals are different than to becoming aware of God, we experience difficulties, a lot of difficulties. Life is trying to tell us that our intentions are wrong. This world is created and is supplied by the one and only Divine Energy. And if anything we do has a different purpose than this Energy, then it is against the flow—against its own nature—and it can never render something good for a long period of time.

Ernest Holmes, the founder of the Science of Mind philosophy, explains in his books that when human beings try to live their life on their own, they get exhausted. But when they realize the power of Divine Energy and align with it, they never get tired, and their life unfolds very differently. Gary Zukav explained the same thing in his book *The Seat of the Soul*. He writes that your life is like a small ship. The energy of the Universe, the energy of God is the Mothership. When you try to go sailing on your own, you get lost, you bump into different obstacles that you feel are destroying you. It's like you try to sail without a GPS, and you easily get knocked off course by whatever comes your way. Isn't it true that a lot of us live our lives that way? Waiting for life to happen to us because it always does manage to knock us off balance.

Well, when we align our lives with the Mothership, as Zukav calls it, and we sail in Her direction, our lives are completely different. The Mothership knows where to take us—knows the best path for us and our growth and evolution. The task is to align with the Mothership by aligning our energy with the energy of God. We do this by first becoming aware of it, then we commune with it so we can understand how to surrender to it. After that, we let our lives unfold in ways that we feel very clueless about in the beginning because it's different than what our egoic mind says is best for life; but if we set our intention to always align with God, things will unfold in incredible ways. We will find unconditional love because that is the ultimate nature, that is the ultimate destination of everything.

By aligning with God, we open ourselves to the nature of the Love Field and its unconditional, beyond-measure appreciation and love for us. Resistance fades away because resistance is only part of believing in the illusions of this world: the illusions that try to prove that we are separate from God. Resistance is an indication of separation from the Divine. The minute you feel any type of resistance, ask yourself, "What am I not seeing? What vision is trying to expose itself to me?"

True vision feels good, liberating, peaceful, calm, and leads to joy. True vision liberates not only you as an individual, but also everyone around you because your vision defines the nature of the people and things around you. In correcting and seeing God, you liberate yourself and everyone, and this happens because there is no separation.

The metaphysical text *A Course in Miracles* teaches that we are not alone in experiencing the effects of our vision. No matter how many times we believe that what we think stays in our heads, it is absolutely not true. Your vision affects everyone and everything. And this is why every time any single person goes in communion with God, it raises the vibration of the entire Earth. We serve as faucets when we open up to the Divine—the Divine pours through us and onto this world. That's why when we live more in illusion than in truth, more in scarcity than in abundance, more in limited thinking than in correct thinking, we deprive our world of Divine Energy. We deprive our consciousness and the consciousness of the world of God.

Ernest Holmes summarized the teachings of Jesus in one phrase: Jesus taught that there is a Fountain of Life from where your life is drawn, and if you will unstop everything in your mind that congests this Fountain, you will be whole. He also talks in his book *Living the Science of Mind* about how we can associate God and ourselves with the body of water in the subterranean levels and the fountains found in the mountains. God is the body of water, and we are the fountains. Some fountains gush forth more water than others, faster or slower than others. There is this pressure under the fountain that causes it to do that. We can associate the pressure with God-pressure, a life force seeking outlet through our thoughts and acts. This beautiful and revealing analogy helps us to understand our roles as outlets of Divine Energy.

Holmes says there are many fountains, many individuals, but only one God-pressured source of all. Jesus also said that the Father that dwelt in Him does all the works, that He by Himself does not do it. We, as fountains, many times block the water coming out with our thoughts, our thinking, our limiting beliefs, and our illusions about ourselves, God, and life. All these illusions are like rocks that collect as debris and block the flow of water through us. We let our fears and doubts make it impossible to let God flow through us.

The problem is not God. It is an illusion that that He is not available, not loving, or forgets about us. God is the River of Life; He always is available and allows life to flow. The problem is with ourselves. We inhibit the flow; we become so afraid that we block all the natural joy that comes from the River of Life.

So, how do we free the way so God can gush through? Through awareness —awareness that feeds us with faith because faith opens us up to the River of Life. It is important to understand that the River of Life is always flowing; it cannot be pushed, dragged, or forced—it can only be allowed. No matter what we want to do, where we want to do it, and with whom we want to do it with, life needs space and freedom to unfold.

Many times, though, we try and force life, whether it be with our career, our relationships, or even our well-being. I remember times when I crafted a to-do list filled with the words: rest, sleep, meditate, yoga. I even added "doing nothing," and I put a time when I would do nothing and for how long. Isn't it crazy when we really think about it? How accustomed have we become to controlling everything? And controlling only blocks the flow of God.

We create all of these lists and we try to control our lives in order to feel in the flow, to feel God, and experience well-being and joy and peace and harmony, but we end up actually doing the opposite. We wind up blocking what we are seeking. We either grasp or become totally indifferent to avoid vulnerability and feeling our essence. The truth is that fear is a portal, just as indifference is a portal—portals to step towards and find what we are looking for in this crazy search for meaning, for purpose, joy, and happiness.

Spirituality is not a thing, teaching, or something "out there;" spirituality is opening up the fountain *within* ourselves. Our mind by itself cannot help us do this; we need to train it to see the truth, to search for the truth. We need to give our mind time and space to get quiet and still, so we can experience the transcendence of ourselves into Divine Energy. Trying to articulate how this happens is not the greatest idea. The intention of this book is to open your mind and consciousness to God, so you can cultivate in yourself thoughts, ideas, and feelings which will bring you closer to your nature, to unlocking your fountain and letting God pour though—through you and through your life. Michael Beckwith once said that you don't need to pray to God, God is praying for you, so you can let Him come forth through you. Prayer is not asking, prayer is allowing. We will discuss prayer more in the second part of this book. But for now, I want to demystify prayer for you. Many people think that God does not know what we need or what is good for us, and we need to pray to tell Him that. God does know all of these things. The purpose of prayer is for you to open yourself to receive them, to clean up the debris in the fountain so that the River of Life can gush through you. In prayer, you make yourself available to God. You clean yourself up, and you make space in your consciousness for all the things you need because God is their only source.

For me to write this book as a first-time author, I had to develop a ritual—a ritual of cleaning the debris so I can let God pour through. I think especially when writing about God, you need to clean yourself up and put yourself to the side for the truth to come forth. Every time before I would write, I meditated and I prayed. I ask God to help me be the channel, the faucet, the fountain that He needs. Writing this book is teaching me an incredible lesson about allowing. I cannot force the words to come through, I cannot think them into phrases. There is a bigger Power that makes them available to me that is from a different place than this life and this world.

I encourage you to try and experience this allowing in whatever you are doing by letting the Universe pour through you. It will feed you with an incredible amount of peace, joy, and purpose. There is no greater feeling, nothing that gives more meaning to our lives, than knowing that we've been used for the highest purpose of the Highest Energy there is on this Earth, in the entire galaxy, and beyond.

The Love Field is the territory where God abides. We feel so great when we experience it because we get glimpses of what Divine Energy really is. Through opening ourselves and becoming the clearest, strongest-gushing fountain, we can let go of our illusions, of our pains, of our fears, and of our attachments. The Love Field dissolves all that is not of His nature. And in the Love Field, we can feel the love, acceptance, and unity with the Highest Power—God.

In the second part of this book, I will teach you how to reach the Love Field in your physical life here on Earth, through your mind, body, and soul. We will explore in-depth methods and processes that can be used to free ourselves by transcending our limited illusion-based egotistic self.

Sometimes we think that our mind has a life of its own, but when we surrender it to God, it will take us places and support us in ways that we couldn't ever imagine. Your mind will become a vehicle for transcendence through the Love Field.

Our bodies—they are temples, temples of God. When you start treating your body this way, it will flourish in the unfoldment of the Divine and bring you into the Love Field.

Your soul is what will expand in beautiful ways in the Love Field. Your soul has been waiting quietly for your awakening; it has been there all along. You will experience the unconditional love of our Creator.

PART II

PRACTICE

CHAPTER 5

RELAXATION

Tension is of this world;
ease is of that in which originates all things.
– Elena Moraru

*P*eace is the opposite of chaos. Love is the opposite of fear. Expansion is the opposite of contraction. And ease is the opposite of tension. All these traits are characteristics of the world within, of the life within, and of the inner environment of the human being. Our external environment does not have to be peaceful for us to feel peaceful. We do not always find ourselves in a place where it's all peace and serenity, but our soul can be at peace, no matter the outside environment.

Usually though, our external environment does follow the signature of our soul after some time, and we begin to find ourselves near people that emanate peace and in places that are full of life and joy. This happens because our external environment reshapes itself based on our state of being; we are reshaping our environment with our energy. This is why peace comes first from within and not from without—the same as love, expansion, and ease.

To experience these states, you do not need to do anything. You do not need seven steps to get what you want, or to go on a mountain, or to buy a house with a garden, or to sign up for a yoga class, or anything else that requires additional things to do. The Love Field is accessible without doing a million things. It is necessary, though, that we understand the Love Field is a place within ourselves that we need to get to. In order to do this, we need to transform from the egocentric identity to the Self that has its being rooted in God.

In this chapter, I want to talk about ease and relaxation. Ease is necessary because when we are at ease it means we are less reactive, we are more centered, and we can see more clearly. When we are at ease, everything unfolds in us with less effort. But how do we bring ourselves to a state of ease and relax ourselves to the degree that we can be more open for the Eternal to reveal itself through us?

Usually, the dis-ease is caused at the level of the mind and body first and then it reaches the soul. But it can also start at the level of the soul and reaches the mind and the body afterwards. For this reason, we will start with a place that is beneficial to both body and mind: nature.

NATURE

We breathe nature, we eat nature, and we drink nature. Our life is constantly supported by the life of nature. I always thought that nature is the greatest therapist there is for your mind, for your body, and for your soul. Because nature is filled with life, it has the potential to heal us and bring more ease into us. Our body becomes very healthy if the majority of what we eat is plants, vegetables, and fruits. Our mind is very healthy if we get enough sunshine and wind and if we look at the sky daily. Looking at the sky is known to help raise your kundalini energy, that dormant energy in the lower part of your torso. When kundalini energy is raised to the upper energy centers in your head and above, you spiritually start to awaken.

Our soul feels light and unburdened if we listen more to the birds, if we nurture animals, and if we treat one another with kindness. Nature has the greatest potential to relax us, destressing our bodies and our minds. Spending a great amount of time outdoors is a requirement if we want to be well—mentally, physically, and spiritually.

Other great ways through which nature brings ease to our lives are caring for plants through gardening, cooking our own food with fresh vegetables, taking care of our soil as much as we can, using herbs and plants as medication as much as possible, and cultivating and growing flowers. Another way to experience nature is to nurture a lot of houseplants and have a home filled with furniture and decor that feels good when you look at it and doesn't stress your brain—a home where it is hard for clutter to gather. Natural beauty is a great healer and nurturer of our soul. Ultimately, taking care of nature as much as we can and respecting the natural habitats of plants and animals is a sacred act. If we take care of nature, nature will take care of us.

Our planet is 70% water—the same as the composition of our bodies. This reveals that we are one with nature; we are so connected with nature that it is impossible that whatever happens to nature does not affect us. The planet has a consciousness of itself, just as we do. The way God has individualized Himself through us, He also did with our planet. Otherwise, there would be no life in it and on it. We are spiritually connected to God through nature as well. God is in the Earth, on the Earth, and above the Earth. The Earth is flourishing with divine energy, but we are just too blind to see this most of the time. Just look at the massiveness of the ocean and wildlife in it, look at the jungles, and at the huge forests expanding over massive lands and countries.

We can also find reassurance in nature's wisdom. Albert Einstein said if we look deeper into nature, we will understand everything better. If we look closely, we can learn great lessons about life in a flower or a tree. Just the fact that everything grows from a tiny seed—an orange comes from an orange tree and not an apple tree—shows that it is the same with us. We are all different, and we cannot expect me to be like you or anyone else. But, at the same time, at our core we have the same source. The difference is only in what we choose to express, which akin to what is ingrained in our seed. Our seed holds what is ingrained in ourselves from when we were in an embryonic state.

As Brice Lipton said, the most experienced life coach you could ever have is nature, she has millions of years of experience managing the entire planet.

Nature can cure almost any sort of problem of the mind and the body if we spend enough time in her presence. The energy of nature has a very powerful impact on the mind and the body and can easily relax both.

MIND

The structure of the human mind has been defined in different ways, depending on the source. Neuroscience and spiritual traditions have shown that the mind is formed by the subconscious, conscious, and superconscious. The subconscious mind is where all the automated processes are regulated from, starting with breathing and ending with emotional reactions to situations. The subconscious mind processes on average 40 million bits of information per second. It is where our long-term memory is stored like past experiences, values, and beliefs. It processes thousands of events at the same time. The subconscious mind is habitual and timeless; it does not understand the notion of time, it understands only the present moment.

The conscious mind has a limited processing capacity of only about 40 bits of information per second. It processes 1–3 events at a time. It is also the place for short-term memory, approximately 20 seconds. It is volitional, sets goals, thinks abstractly, and judges the results. The conscious mind is also bounded to time, past or future.

The superconscious mind is the place of the Higher Self and has an infinite, non-linear processing with unlimited speed and capacity. It is where we receive our spiritual guidance. The superconscious mind sees the big picture of your life and helps to ensure that your goals are both safe and appropriate in the context of your life's purpose.

It is important to be aware of the nature of our mind. What happened for the last ten years of my life was a process of awakening to the superconscious mind. Ten years ago, I had no idea of what my mind does, how my thoughts create my life, and how my subconscious programming is literally reflected in every decision, every action, and every intention. Through contemplation, meditation, prayer, and the process of seeking something to fulfill me, I have come to the realization that I have a superconscious mind and I am not alone in this life—there is a power with me that reassures me that I am divinely guided and protected.

Some of us may not realize it, but the reason that a lot of stuff in our lives does not work out is for our own good. We try different things, and the majority of what we consciously try to do encounters a lot of resistance.

For a long time, I thought there was something wrong with me because things were not working out. But when I stepped back and looked from a broader view, I realized that very big things did happen for me without much resistance, like moving across two continents and an ocean to start a new life. I did not push this to happen, it somehow happened by itself. I realized if such a big move can be directed and happen without me making a thousand goals and a million vision boards then what hadn't worked out until now was probably for my best and highest interest.

Even in my last career path, I wanted so badly to be a successful interior designer who had her own flourishing practice. I did open my practice, but there was always something holding me back from stepping into the next level. At some point, I thought maybe I lacked confidence. Now I realize it was not my confidence issues. (After all, I do have the courage to write a book about God, so I think I have a pretty good amount of confidence.) The reasons were not tied to my lack of skills or confidence, but to the fact that my purpose for my life was not aligned with God's purpose for my life. If I had stayed in that practice, you would not be reading this book. If it wasn't for Divine Energy wanting me to write and publish this book, I would be doing something else with my life right now.

A great way to stop the build-up of resistance in our mind is to stop wanting to make things happen and surrender, give up, and let go. Many of us will find this solution terrifying, but it is incredibly liberating. You see, no matter what we will try to tell ourselves, the nature of the universe is not based upon what our ego knows and wants. We can try to control the outcome as much as we want, but what I realized is that things are not happening because we want to manifest them. We want them, that's true, but a Greater Power needs to want them too.

Recently, I had to relearn this when for some reason a flight that I rebooked because of the pandemic would not finalize. It was a very weird situation, and the airline just couldn't do it. I was so frustrated at first that I even told a friend I am sick of life lessons or whatever the Universe is trying to teach me. But I realized that everything happening was not by my own doing, and it is backed by the Greatest Power. I instantly started to feel gratitude when I thought about it this way—gratitude to God for wanting me to have a child and giving this incredible gift to me, gratitude for all the things that did not work out that I wanted, gratitude that I have a family, and gratitude that my parents and siblings are alive and healthy. And ultimately, I realized that I am so grateful for God wanting to give this life to me and send me here on Earth.

Nothing that is happening in our lives is because we just think about it, plan it, and do it. This is necessary, but ultimately it works out if God wants it to work out. It would be foolish for us to believe that we are completely alone in manifesting our life. Complete surrender releases us from the strain of trying to achieve things and helps us relax and allows our life to unfold by what God has in His plan for us. When we let go of the outcome, we allow God to fully emerge in our life because we understand and trust His power and presence in ourselves.

The mind is the main part of ourselves that can go very easily into dis-ease from overthinking. One way to bring ease to your mind is to take your daily to-do lists and remove a lot of stuff from them. It is okay to have a day with only two items on the list, or with even no items.

Another way to ease your mind is to schedule days in your life where you talk only with people that you know will not give you the news report. Many times, speaking with others can clutter your mind with events that are not related to you. While it's important to listen to what others have to say, sometimes you need a break to find the quietness of your mind. It is okay to take days when you unplug and do not even utter a word from your mouth. I would have silent days almost every day if I could. I love the effect on my mind and my body of the days when I don't speak at all in general. It's like a rejuvenating restart of my entire system. This being said, I do love to talk and to talk with people; but if I don't take a break, I burn out incredibly easily. It's valuable to learn how to set the boundaries that bring your mind peace.

BODY

The body is such a magnificent and miraculous creation. Some people call it a miracle when a severe disease disappears on its own; I call it a miracle every time I cut my finger

64

and within a day I see how the skin is pulling to heal the wound. Who does that? Who is in the body that makes it so incredible at healing itself? I have but one word for it and by now you probably know what it is: God. The body is a self-healing, self-adapting vehicle. It is the vehicle for our spirit, for our soul; it is the vehicle for the God within us.

We live many times with such judgmental attitudes towards our bodies—that it should look a certain way, that it should work out in a certain amount of time with a certain amount of resistance, that it should never age, and most commonly, it should always feel good.

The body has intelligence. If it's not working properly, the cause is not that it is defective, but that we are doing something that interferes with its natural laws. When we interfere, the natural cycles are being disturbed, and then the body sends messages through symptoms and diseases that something needs to be adjusted. This could be the need for adjustment in our external environment, caused by the conditions we work and live in, or of our internal environment caused by our thoughts, the food we put in our bodies, and the movement that we engage in.

The most recent realization I had was that if the body is not well, I will not be well mentally and spiritually. The body needs to be in balance for us to experience life truthfully. And if the body is not in balance, then we need to get it there.

Our body reflects our state of mind through how the levels in hormones, other chemical elements, and our muscles react to our thoughts. In the book *Biology of Belief*, Bruce Lipton talks about the incredible link between our belief system and our biology. Genes are not the cause of diseases or disturbances in our bodies. It is our minds that create health or disease.

The things we carry in our mind, especially our subconscious mind and the things we choose to believe about ourselves, about others, and about life, either condition us to be and stay healthy or the opposite. Your thoughts and emotions make you sick or make you healthy. I am convinced of this being true, and if you are not, try and investigate people who are healthy and people who are not. Do not investigate their lifestyle, but rather, investigate the nature of their mind and what's going on in their heads from the morning to the night.

I find it very easy to get out of balance physiologically. If we are not very aware, we continue to feel strain and contraction in our body until it starts breaking down. That's why it's important to pay attention. If you feel your back is very tight, you can get acupuncture or do stretching to help it, yet the main cause for the tension in the body is not in the body, but in the mind. You need to resolve the tension in the mind. Having a healthy state of mind is a prerequisite for a healthy body. Of course, it is still necessary to eat healthily and move your body often. When you are in a healthy state of mind, this is exactly what you want to do: eat healthily and move your body in healthy ways.

The relaxation of the body starts with the relaxation of the mind. The relaxation of the mind starts with a relaxed internal soul state. The soul needs to be at peace in order for the mind to be at peace, so then the body can be at peace. The soul is at peace only when it becomes aware of its Divine Nature and of the Divine Presence in it.

The body is temporary, and this is important to understand. The physical is not the only thing there is. Behind the body, behind any material representation of any kind, rests the eternal—the Essence that is at the core of everything, the Divine Energy that cannot be changed, transformed, destroyed, or hurt. This is who we are, we are creations of the Divine, we are children of the Most High. God is in us and in everything. To look at our bodies as something holy with a holy purpose—to carry the Most High in them on this Earth—conditions us to awake to a different vision when we look at our bodies. We need to respect them exactly the way they are. No matter if our bodies look perfect based on society's ideas or not, they are still perfect because they carry the perfect Divine Energy in them and this makes them perfect.

A Course in Miracles teaches that God is in everything, in us, and in everything we see. We see separation and do not see God in everything; this is the reason that we feel so much pain and suffering. When we open and train ourselves to see everything as holy because it is filled with the divine essence of God, then a grandiose respect and appreciation blooms inside ourselves for everything around us and in us, including our bodies.

Our attachment to our physical body and obsession with it are indications of our separation from God. We have forgotten who we are; we have forgotten God again. When the memory of our Creator sprouts again in our mind, we forget the attachment, we forget the obsession, because we know that who we are is not the body.

We are spiritual beings living a human experience. This has been said by many, but I think a lot of people do not understand the essence of this powerful statement. As a spiritual being, we understand that there is an Energy in our body that did not come from the body or from anything material. This Energy is what is called our spiritual nature. It is beyond time and space and anything physical; it is eternal, is never born, and never dies. The body is only a vehicle for this Energy. If we contemplate this enough, we will find relief and peace in a lot of our turbulences.

SOUL

What is the soul? Many times we talk about the soul as something very static. However, I understand it as something very dynamic. There is movement, there is energy, there is life in it. The soul is life itself. This invisible Energy that gives life to the body grows the flowers and the trees and moves the Earth around the Sun, just as it gives life to our souls. The soul is expansion. The soul feels at its worst when confined and restricted. It needs to always expand because this is its nature.

In a lot of my meditations, I got to an internal state of emptiness that I can't define in any way. I am just sitting on the floor, but something is going on in the structure of my attention and my perception of myself. One time, I felt that my body was so large that I could fill entire galaxies and universes in it. It was like sitting in the cosmos. The Earth felt like a tiny, dark ball that looked the size of a small star we see as we watch the sky at night.

I haven't told a lot of people about this experience because it felt weird to describe it. I started to have this vision when I was a child. Today, I understand what it means. I enter my soul and my limitless mind, and I can perceive at a somehow higher level of consciousness the expansion of my being.

Perceiving the soul consciously gives us an intellectual experience of it. When the mind sees the soul, it sees itself as something particularly large. But when we feel the soul, that's when the nature of it shows itself to us because we understand the depth of things through a different perception than only our five senses.

It is hard to define the soul, I would say quite impossible. In my understanding, I find the soul as a mixture of energy, consciousness, and being. We understand what is energy and we understand what is consciousness, but what is being? I think concerning "being," you can only experience the word, as intellectually it is not definable. Being is existing. The soul exists, it never dies, is never born. The body is born and the body dies, but what is inside the body is eternal. The soul is eternal.

After I started to study *A Course in Miracles*, I realized that the soul is the energy of Christ within us, the energy of the Son of God. Then I started to ask questions. When we are deluded by illusions of this world, who is the one that perceives the world, who sees lack and limitation, despair, and depression and war? The answer that came through was that this happens when the mind tries to create a self of its own. When the mind creates a self of its own, it thinks it is separate from everything, exists independently in the body, and there is nothing else besides itself. But there is. The soul is in the body too, not only the mind.

69

The intellectual mind has created a separate self, many call this identity the ego self. The ego consists of the ideas in our mind that what exists is only what we can see with our two eyes. The ego believes that who we are is only this mind with which we can think. No wonder *A Course in Miracles* calls the separation from God an illusion. This is because it's a manufacturing of the mind disregarding the spirit inside us. The truth is that we are more than the mind: we are also the soul. The soul feels, the soul knows the truth, and the soul never wants to be separate. The soul always loves and connects because it is already connected to everything. The soul knows God because it comes from God, it is the Son of God. Through the soul, we can access the Eternal inside us. Through the soul, we can find and communion with God. Through the soul, we can find freedom. Through the soul, we can find liberation from everything.

First, we need to understand what the soul is. Second, we need to pay attention to ourselves and look within ourselves and find our soul, find the Christ within. Then third, we live our life from that place. To live this material and physical life from that spiritual place within us means we have found our soul. This spiritual place is where love, compassion, forgiveness, and total surrender exist. It is in us—in all of us. Our function on this Earth is to become aware and live our life from this place within.

We often use the phrases, "Oh, my soul hurts. My soul is not at peace. My heart is in turmoil." The truth is that none of these are actually true. The soul can never be hurt or tormented. It is our consciousness that is battling between two worlds—the world of the soul and the world of the ego.

When we are in turmoil and we seek peace, it usually means that we have deviated from that sacred place within; we have given space in our consciousness to the ideas of our ego self.

One situation I want to bring up so we can understand these ideas better is a situation when you have problems in the relationship with your life partner. Many times we battle in our mind, and we cannot find peace because we think if we care about ourselves then our life partner suffers. The other option is if we care about them, we suffer. Let's say you have a child together, handling tasks can be a very hard thing to do. Many times both partners are sleep deprived and both feel like the other one is doing too little because they are just so exhausted all the time. The issue is not that one or the other doesn't do enough. It is because there is just too much to handle and no matter how involved one or the other might be, things will still feel exhausting because there is just too much on the table.

In this particular case, two things happen for us internally. One, we do a lot and feel tired, and we get the impression that the other one is not doing enough, so we feel frustrated and abused. It feels like we are lacking appreciation from the other person. Two, we give up and stop doing some things, but internally we still feel bad and guilty; this time because we feel we are not doing enough, and we put things on the other person's shoulders.

In both cases, we are in turmoil, and many times we feel there is just no way out. There is no way for you to be at peace because you either exhaust yourself or you get some rest but feel incredibly guilty. In this case, how can we enter our soul

71

and be at complete peace? Surrender! It is the hardest thing to do, but it is the best thing to do.

You just let go, sort of like giving up. You let go of doing things you cannot do, and you let go of wanting to control the outcome of your relationship. If things will go crazy, let them go. If you might end up separating, let it be. After all, the truth is we cannot control a lot of things, but we can control how well we go back to ourselves and let peace abide within us by completely letting go.

CONTEMPLATION

In Christianity, contemplation refers to a content, free mind directed towards the awareness of God as a living reality. In some other traditions, contemplation is seen as when the heart and the mind reconcile into one thing. Others spiritual traditions have said that through contemplation, we can keep the truth about life and God alive.

What I think about contemplation is that it is a first step for someone who has not acknowledged God before to come into contact with Him. In contemplation, we become accustomed with the nature of our human side and understand the limitations of it in order to transcend it. In contemplation, we witness ourselves—who we are when we are part of the illusion, and who we are when we communion with God.

Contemplation is a process of also acknowledging the spiritual nature of life. We become aware that who we thought we were before contemplation is very different than who we truly are. We realize our life is not that of a human being, but a life of a spiritual being. We start to see our soul in contemplation, and we become so interested in it because we've never experienced the nature of it. The soul becomes even more exciting to understand when we see it as the source of our joy and happiness.

In contemplation we ask questions, lots of questions. The answers might reveal themselves to us instantaneously or take a moment or a day, but they come. When you sit in contemplation—on the floor, in a church or a garden, or even at our desk—Spirit starts moving around you and in you. Spirit starts enveloping you with an energy that you've never felt before.

Contemplation is not just for people new to discovering their soul and God. Contemplation is a practice of awareness for any kind of person. In this process, we step on the threshold of the Kingdom of God. In contemplation, we learn how to enter our soul, the most peaceful place within us. When we experience our soul, nothing feels the same anymore. We learn that we can retreat into it whenever we lose ourselves in chaos, and it becomes a place of relief and rejuvenation. No wonder some people say when you feel you are losing it, just close your eyes and enter the peace that you already are. Chaos is in our minds; and if we transcend our mind, we find only peace and emptiness, ease and comfort.

Contemplation is a process that can be used anywhere and anytime. It is easy and fast. You don't even have to close your eyes. It is a tool to come back to the truth and escape illusion. I consider it different from meditation and prayer because in its nature, it differs in practice and accessibility.

Contemplation helps us instantly have access to the Divine. We can be doing anything and just stop and sit for a moment and imagine the presence of the Divine around us, and then we are there—we are entering the soul. We are entering a place of more clarity, more peace, and more tranquility.

I call contemplation the time when the thought of God enters the mind. During the day, we can set our intention to remember to sit in contemplation a couple of moments here and there. We should do this without thinking about time, because we can enter contemplation at any moment, even if it's just tiny moments.

We can also sit in contemplation for hours. Contemplation trains us to get into meditation, so we can then enter prayer, which we will cover in the next chapters. When we learn to sit in contemplation, glimpses of the Kingdom of God start to be seen. It is marvelous to taste the Kingdom of the Most High. Inspiration, abundance, and unconditional love are only steps away in our consciousness.

A Course in Miracles teaches that the Word of God is written on our mind and His awareness on our heart. Through contemplation, meditation, and prayer, we can understand the Word of God, become aware of Him, commune with Him and embrace a spiritual life. Now that we've covered contemplation, it's time to move on to meditation.

CHAPTER 6

MEDITATION

"Please enter where You already abide. May my mind and heart be pure and true, and may I not deviate from the things of goodness."
– Marianne Williamson

*W*hen I think of meditation, there is this beautiful feeling blooming in my chest. Meditation has saved me, literally, from all the crises in my life. I found meditation accidentally when I started to practice yoga. A friend of mine had back problems, so she took me with her to her yoga class. Then while searching for more information online about yoga, I came across meditation courses. I gave it a try in 2013 and have never stopped since then.

Meditation has been portrayed in the media as a practice of sitting still and getting comfortable with silence. There are even apps today that bring meditation to the public as a practice of the mind, where you quiet your mind. While this is in part of what meditation is, it is not the essence of it. Meditation is a spiritual practice, where the goal is finding God, no matter if you are aware of it or not.

When you practice meditation just as a mindfulness practice, where you try and calm your mind or are guided to think about the ocean and relax your muscles, you get just that—the relaxation of your body. But meditation is not intended to only relax the body or quiet our mind. Meditation is the prescription for communion with God.

When I started meditation, the practice that I started with was Sahaja Yoga. Sahaja Yoga is a meditation where you practice the awakening of your kundalini energy. I had no idea at the time; I just loved the relaxation and the peacefulness that I would acquire from practicing it. Later, I started to find out what this kundalini awakening is—the path to find God within; it is the path to self-realization. Meditation is the steppingstone towards prayer, and prayer ultimately consists of building stones for communion with the Divine.

PRACTICE

The practice of meditation is pretty simple. I know there are millions of types of meditations out there. It can be confusing at times to try to figure out which one would work best for you. But I think the greatest things in the universe are simple, and so is meditation. Depending on what type of person you are, no matter if you practiced meditation before, I recommend ten minutes in the morning and ten minutes in the evening. If both of these times are hard, just pick any other times during the day. The time doesn't matter as much; what matters is that you do it two times a day.

With time, you can gradually increase it to three times a day. Three times a day is perfect. It is the ideal way to train your mind to meditate as a habit. When you start practicing for several weeks, you will naturally want to increase those ten minutes to more minutes, and you can meditate for as long as you want, but not less than ten minutes.

The room you are sitting in needs to be quiet, and you need to be alone. Some people love having relaxing music in the background while sitting in meditation, but some people don't. I particularly like to sit in silence without any music. It doesn't matter if you choose to meditate with music, but if you do, make sure to select something very relaxing that will not bring up thoughts or emotions for you. For example, for me, piano music brings nostalgic thoughts to my mind, so I don't play it in general that often overall.

So how do you meditate? The simplest way to meditate is to sit on the floor, chair, or a sofa with your legs crossed. Your spine needs to sit erect straight, but also be relaxed and not strained.

While you sit, start becoming aware of your breath. Focus on the breath, filling and emptying your lungs while you breathe in and out. Start becoming aware of your mind and your state of being, how you feel, how thoughts are coming and going, and just sit there and observe. And that's it, that's how you meditate, you just sit, relax, and breathe.

Meditation is simple, and it needs to be simple, otherwise, it interferes with what unfolds within you during meditation, which is what you make space for when you meditate. Our crazy lifestyles are bringing into our life the opposite of peace and joy and happiness. But when we start meditating, we slowly bring back what's natural for us—a natural way to live by becoming more present, by slowing down our pace, and by making space within us for God to unfold.

The practice of meditation becomes a no-practice after a while. After some time, if you meditate regularly, you will find yourself drifting into a meditative state anywhere and on-demand instantly. This is the power of habit and regular practice. When that happens, you forget that you have a meditation practice, and meditation just becomes a way of life. You learn to excuse yourself when you slip away and get into a chaotic state of being to go and collect yourself and bring back your attention to what is true, focusing on the spirit inside you. So don't feel intimidated when I mention the word practice—meditation will not be just another thing to do on your to-do list. In the beginning, it might, but if you keep at it, it will gradually become a natural way of being for you and you will seek every free minute to use for it.

There's many neuroscience studies which prove the extraordinary, physical, mental, and spiritual benefits of meditation. You can google this for yourself. There are enough studies to convince you that if you want to live better, you can meditate. The best-selling author and spiritual teacher, Gabby Bernstein, once said that the secret to her great life is that she meditates, and many more like her have said the same.

Meditation has had an incredible impact on my life. The person I was when I started meditating has completely transformed over the years. I was a very shy young woman who was raised in a small village in one of Europe's smallest countries. I was brought up during the transition from the Soviet Union to an independent Communist country.

Growing up in Communism shapes you specifically differently than when you are not born in Communism. As a child that got through an educational system that left me with serious emotional and psychological traumas, after graduating high school and then university, I found myself living in a complete survival mode on an emotional and spiritual level. Then I decided to move to America, which I'd been made to believe that things worked differently and life was supposed to be easier. Well, for me, it did not turn out like that. This is the same for many other immigrants in America.

Many people think that material and economic abundance has something to do with emotional and spiritual abundance in the way that if you have the first, the second comes automatically. That is definitely not true. I was too young at the time to know because, unfortunately, no one taught me that. We teach children to seek success, but many times we miss on explaining to them what success means exactly.

So when I moved to America, I felt like someone had dropped me from a helicopter in the middle of the Pacific Ocean with no life jacket. Well, my life jacket was revealed to me after a couple of years of trying to stay on the surface like a non-swimmer. My life jacket was meditation.

God had thrown it at me successfully. After meditation came into my life, everything changed. The Elena born and raised in Moldova has become a new Elena—an Elena that is not conditioned by her upbringing anymore, even though it helped her become who she is today. Today, I know God. Today, I know that I have the power to choose how to see life and the world. Today, I know that what I choose to cultivate inside myself will shape the outer world around me. Today, I know that only God can save you and lift you from the darkest room you are in. Today, I know that the purpose of life is not to live well or have some material success, but to find all the reassurances you are seeking inside yourself, to become aware of your divine nature, to become aware of the Truth. And all this knowledge has come about because of me clicking on a play button on a very humble-looking website ten years ago. All of this knowledge is because of meditation.

There are other practices that fall under the category of meditation. For example, recently I became familiar with self-hypnosis—not the self-hypnosis videos on YouTube, but rather the 7th Path Self-Hypnosis developed by a well-known hypnotist in Dallas, Texas. It is a particular type of self-hypnosis and only a certified hypnotist can train you how to do it correctly.

I've talked about hypnotherapy in a previous chapter, but I want to bring it up again because it is changing my life in significant ways. If you go and do any type of therapy, I recommend you quit and go and do hypnotherapy for several sessions. It will change the way you view therapy in general, and it will fix the problems you have in several sessions that with regular therapy take years to fix.

I consider the 7th Path Self-Hypnosis a kind of meditation, but one that changes your life at an exponential level in a short amount of time because in this meditation you rewrite the programs that are running your life. In this particular type of self-hypnosis, you get to carefully adjust the suggestions based on what problem you have and what you are willing, open, and looking to change. The best part of is that you program your subconscious mind with natural divine ideas where the Highest Power that you believe in is involved in correcting your vision about yourself, your life, and God.

The greatest thing that you realize when you do this particular type of meditation is that no matter what your mind was trained to think about God, when you practice the recognition of God, your whole body, brain, mind, and being goes into total relaxation. You feel filled with ease and grace and love, it just feels so natural for us to acknowledge the existence and the presence of God. You can find more about 7th Path Self-Hypnosis here: www.7thpathselfhypnosis.com.

When I started to meditate, I started with guided meditations, another form of meditation. Guided meditations are great for beginners who are very unfamiliar with meditation. Still, even as I say this, the best way to meditate is with the simple practice described at the beginning of this chapter.

The guided meditations that I started with were from the Sahaja Yoga Meditation website. I started with Sahaja Yoga because I googled "online meditation" and www.onlinemeditation.org came up. I clicked the link, and I found meditation sessions for free. And that's how I began. The sessions were 8 minutes each, so it was very doable at the beginning, when I was sitting but my whole body and mind wanted to get up and do something. This is why I recommend starting with 10 minutes, or even 8 minutes as I did.

Over the years, I tried many other types of meditations, and I found out that what's out there are mostly practices that feel very sterile. Even the Headspace app, which I use now and then, is not the best. I find those meditations to be more like exercises for mental and physical relaxation. Meditation is not a mental exercise. The relaxation and the release of mental and physical tension is one of the beneficial results, but the purpose of meditation is to find God. No matter what is being advertised to you, this is the truth about meditation.

So try the simple practice, see how you are doing with it, and have patience. If you are curious about the other types of meditation I mentioned, check them out and practice them for some time. Eventually, you will understand which one is best for you now. And in a month, you might want to change things up a little bit. But remember, the simpler the better, and the easier it is to keep doing it.

SILENCE

A Course in Miracles teaches that when we are in turmoil, we need to sit quietly, for quietness is the end of strife and the journey to peace. To sit quietly when we feel an internal storm is ravaging us is no easy task. No wonder everyone says if you feel a tsunami inside, just sit. Just sit and patiently wait in the middle of it. When you do that, peace is inevitable. I picture myself sitting in a cross-legged pose in the middle of the vortex of my internal storm while all around me feels like a racking hell.

At the same time, this nonaction attitude is very liberating because you know you cannot do anything until everything quiets down. As a result of sitting, silence prevails. Silence is a state of complete surrender. Silence makes itself available within us when we have completely let ourselves in the hands of our divine essence. In meditation, we do this almost all the time.

When we quiet ourselves, or try and become mindful of what's going on within us, we are handing our power from the ego to our soul. The way silence blooms in us is by removing all the resistance to other things, and when all resistance is removed, all that is left is a deep sense of peace. Peace needs silence in order to abide within us.

The truth is that we all are seeking the place of silence within us. Because in silence, our true nature has space to reveal itself. In silence, we are not being pulled to the right or the left. In silence we are in the middle, still and unshakable. This stillness helps us see the illusions of this world in a very clear, unobscured view.

I love silence. I also love going into environments where a lot is going on, but if I do not come back to a place of silence and peace very quickly by retreating into my own private space, I lose myself. I know for some of us, the introverts, sitting comfortably in silence is not as hard as for some of us who are extroverts.

I have an extrovert in my life, one of my closest people. Since she started meditation, she is having a much easier time sitting still and being okay with silence. Many times, she describes moments of loneliness, even if she is with two people around her. She is engaging and connecting with them, but not as in the case when people are together, and she feels very lonely because they do not interact with each other at the level they wish for.

If you are an extrovert, you still naturally love silence, and it is not an unnatural thing. I think that what extroverts are more prone to is using socializing and getting energy from their external environment for stimulation to such a degree that they lose insight of what's going on within them. When this happens, psychological and emotional traumas or painful memories get buried deep inside without processing or even knowing they are there. And because the extrovert is in such a continuous process of being everywhere with everyone, they lose themselves in the external identity and it becomes harder to sit in silence. Because when extroverts sit in silence, all the stuff deep in their psyche, which was unknown until then, starts coming to the surface. When this happens, sitting in silence for some time is very painful. But getting through this pain is the only way out—the way to true peace and serenity.

Silence is such an incredible gift. Its nature is liberating. Resistance dissolves in silence. Some may say that silence is the state where there is nothing. And the state where there is nothing is a state that we crave. Because only in nothingness do we liberate ourselves, and we do that by realizing that the true road to freedom is not somewhere out there. It does not come by being and doing, rather it is in this nothingness that we let go completely. When we let go completely, we become free. We realize that freedom is not something we grasp, but it is something we surrender ourselves to.

When we become quiet enough to enter into silence, we become aware of our power, of our power to liberate ourselves. This power is not in the hands of anyone; it is in our own being. We hold the power to let go, to disengage from resistant thoughts, to surrender and become empty. And in this emptiness, we find our freedom.

The thing about silence is that we need to go into it often in order to train ourselves to enter it on demand. Some of us may feel that it is so hard to live in our own minds because they are filled with everything. The solution is to make time to sit still without distractions in an environment where you can become aware of your breath and your body and let everything else go—even for just a couple of moments. If we do this often, we train our mind, our body, and our entire being to find this space that we can enter all the time, where everything melts away. After some time, there will be incredible things happening. Remember, silence is a steppingstone towards greater awareness, awareness of yourself and ultimately of God within you.

In silence, we make space within us for the things that we don't have time and attention for on a regular basis. Only in these moments of silence do we make space for love within us and in our lives. We live these crazy lives sometimes. We run everywhere, taking care of everything and everyone, and we forget so much in this insane process; we forget about the most important thing of all—we forget about love. We become so mechanical at living our lives that only when we make time to pause and breathe do we realize how much we have deviated from our own nature, how much we have deviated from feeling and being love. You see, feeling and being love is not something conditioned from outside of us; it is something that exists in our own nature.

In silence, love springs up again from within our hearts and nourishes us so that we go into the world and start nourishing others again.

There are many ways to make going into silence a habit. One is to take every opportunity to sit quietly with yourself. If closing your eyes will help you, then do that. Let nature help you too; find spaces in nature where you can sit undisturbed. Use daily activities as reminders to sit in silence. For example, before any meal, sit with your food in front of you and thank the Universe that you have food to eat. After that, surrender to the moment, sit with yourself for a minute or so in silence and then start your meal. Do this before and after you've eaten.

For me, as a mom of a toddler, when my daughter is home, it is hard to sit quietly when she is not napping—I would say it is impossible. So when she naps or goes to bed at night, I make sure I disconnect from everything and sit for as much time as possible. My evenings have become my holy hours. I meditate, I pray, I read, and I surrender as much as I can. When I don't do that, I either sleep poorly or have a hard time going to bed.

Sitting in silence can be hard when we are having a busy day, or when our mind is racing at such a high speed that we barely can stop ourselves to drink some water. I am a person who is prone to become trapped into this busyness a lot. One day, I started questioning why I am so anxious when there are a million things to do. What I realized was that I was subconsciously used to functioning in fear, in worry, and wanting to be in control.

When this happens, it is a sign that we are living in fear and without God. Only when we feel separate from our divinity do we start acting frantically and anxious. We are not built to believe we have everything in our control or to control everything intellectually. We are built to lean on Someone greater than us—Someone more powerful than our ego mind. When we learn to lean in and surrender, our life becomes like a river, flowing in the right direction without trying to force anything. Changing the habits of our subconscious is not an easy task. But we do not have to do it alone; we can let God do it for us. Through prayer and meditation, we can surrender and transform our neuroses into Divinity.

PRESENCE

Our daily thinking patterns have become so addictive because of the complex lifestyles we create. There is always something to distract our attention. If we do not pay attention, we can get hooked on thinking for days, weeks, and months without taking a break—without taking a breath, literally. Thinking suppresses our breathing process. When we think anything, we become unconscious of our breathing. Only by sitting in silence can we break the cycle.

In silence, we can become aware of our thoughts. When we become aware of them, something shifts. We become conscious that there is this place within where thoughts do not enter; they simply feel like clouds coming and going. In this place within, we start breathing freely for the first time. In this place within, we find the true presence of ourselves, of the Universe, and of God. This true presence of ourselves, of our being, having its nature in God feels nurturing, easy, light, loving, and free.

Since I became a mother, having time to sit in silence has become tricky. Now that my daughter is already a toddler, things are getting better in that regard. After some life experience, you can understand and accept who you are. I believe any person needs time for themselves, no matter if you are a very social individual or someone that enjoys a quieter life. I came to understand as I mentioned in previous chapters that I am a person who needs a lot of time in silence. It is where I gather myself, where I find peace with myself, with life's challenges, and with God.

In my many years of struggle and crises, the only place where I could find relief, freedom, and redemption was within. Today I live by being very conscious of the fact that no matter where I go, no matter what status I get, or what kind of people are around me, these things all do the same: they come and go. Only the true Presence of my being and God within me never leaves, never transforms. It is always present, always loving, and always filled with all that I need.

You probably have heard it many times that all you need is within you. It is absolutely true. The source of all things is in God, in our divine essence—no matter if it's physical, emotional, or spiritual. God is the first cause of all things. In this Presence within us, we can find the root of our problems and also the solutions to them.

In meditation, we become comfortable with feeling and staying present to this Presence within us; I call it the most marvelous place. It is where I find my absolute peace and freedom. And I try to live from that place. This Presence reveals to us our true nature. We are never bound by anything; there is nothing that this presence does not dissolve. Any problem is all part of a reality that does not encompass our true nature.

For example, in a situation where you have a family member you would like to really get along with, but it feels impossible at times, your ego might tell you that this is really bad. Your ego will try to convince you that life is unfair for having someone that you love disagreeing with you so much. But if you sit silently and enter that space within you that knew the problem before you even became conscious of it, it will tell you and reassure you of great things that will liberate you from your attachment to this situation.

You will understand that it is not in your power to change people. This is not your job, and you shouldn't want to do that for your own benefit. It is okay to disagree. Even if you cannot change the relationship with that family member, there is a reason that you disagree. This person is probably disagreeing with you so something within you can transform; that weak part of you that became emotionally dependent on that person and of their acceptance of you can disappear. This is how you find freedom—you find it in the truth. And the truth is that nothing will ever fill you, will ever make you as content and peaceful, as the Divine Presence which exists within you.

Our divine presence within us reveals to us the true presence of God. Jesus did say that the Kingdom of God is not somewhere, but it is within us. Yet for some reason, a lot of us are still looking for it outside ourselves—in relationships, in careers, in business, and even in churches.

Recently I came back from Europe, where I spent a month with my extended family. Since we live so far away from each other, we needed more time to catch up and enjoy each other's presence. During this trip, I had no space to sit in silence or meditate, and not as much intimacy as I am used to with my wonderful, peaceful life in America. My father owns a small vineyard on a beautiful hillside and that is where I often went to center myself. I am telling you about this experience because a lot of us live like that—with no time to meditate, to sit in silence. We just go about our lives in chaos, filled with fear and uncertainty.

When I came back from my trip, the joints in my entire body were hurting, not because of some health or weather problem, but because of not breathing properly, not resting properly, and not sitting in meditation and prayer as I usually sit. I realized for the hundredth time that every individual is fully responsible for creating their life. You can choose chaos, or you can choose harmony. You can choose to live agitated, distracted, and reactive, or you can choose to live peacefully, calm, and present. It is a choice. God's presence is within us all. Calmness and serenity are within; love and freedom are within.

When we start practicing meditation, there is really no place to go; the place will reveal itself to you if you sit often enough. The Presence that is full of peace, tranquility, life, and freedom is available within a split second in your consciousness. Make silence your daily friend. If you feel lonely when you are alone, start to question what are you actually afraid of. What's inside you that is so uncomfortable? Look deep into those things because usually behind them you will find treasures of the truth. And in those treasures, the magnificent presence of God will reveal itself to you.

TRANSCENDENCE

What usually happens during meditation after you practice for a while is that you start to transcend your regular states of consciousness. Meaning, you start to go beyond your regular ways of thinking. You might still have the same thinking patterns, but you are aware of them, and new ones start to emerge. To transcend means to go through and beyond something—to transform a state of being by going beyond it and letting whatever is beyond it emerge.

Usually, behind any negative state of being, a very positive and uplifting energy resides. The negativity is only like a veil, it is some sort of illusionary state that we are in at times. This is the reason that these illusionary states start disappearing and you and your life become more peaceful, calmer, more centered and more fulfilled when you practice meditation.

I have done the meditation that started the idea for this book, Michael Beckwith's meditation where I encountered the Love Field, and I am still practicing it today. I experience something different every time. New states of consciousness emerge while doing it, and lots of wisdom is being revealed to me.

In one session, I experienced a deep state of calm and tranquility. But I also have realized states that I was not accustomed to being in, and the idea of them sounded very attractive to me. And what I've done through many years of meditation has been to try to enter them—that's right, try! I was not able to enter them at first because the nature of who I was inside was not allowing me. Inside, I was someone who never believed that calm and tranquility are a good state to be in, because if I was calm and tranquil, for me meant to be slow—moving slowly, doing things slowly, and never being in a hurry.

I grew up around agitated women, who worked hard, fast, and efficient. There was no other way to do life because that was the only way to survive. You had to move fast to live a decent life when there were no dishwashers, washing machines, or the ability to get a housekeeper. I realized in my meditation session that I have inherited these ideas of always being hurried, always doing things fast. I thought, the faster the better, as that way I could accomplish a lot of things during a certain amount of time.

When I started my first job in America, I remember being praised for working so efficiently and fast. I was called a very hardworking girl. My friends were the same. We even discussed how slow some of our co-workers were, wondering how in the world they secured their jobs by being like that. And the thing is, when I started to meditate and embrace a slower way of life, I still struggled. Even today, sometimes I have to force myself to quiet down.

What I've realized is that this hurry and speed in doing things reveals a lot of worries that I carry in my consciousness, a lot of distrust about how life will unfold. My mother used to say, "How can I enjoy sitting around when there is so much to do?" And I totally understood her because living in a rural area in Eastern Europe with three children, a fulltime job, and no housekeeper, there was literally no time to sit around. But her children grew up, my mother moved to a city area in Italy, and she still has trouble sitting around.

Tranquility and calm are a natural state of our being. The nature of God is tranquil and calm; it is a state of feeling secure and protected. When I was contemplating this idea of being completely safe and protected, calmness and tranquility unfolded inside myself. I was transcending worry and fear and entering a state of being loved and taken care of.

I tried to expand this state. It was not an easy thing to do, because in that moment, I realized how entangled I was with my ideas of being fast and efficient. Questions like this came to mind: "How can I calm down when I need to do this, and this, and this? Is it even safe to calm down? Wouldn't I lose something or forget to do something or get too relaxed that I completely neglect other things that can bring me happiness?"

Little did I know that in that very moment, in that tranquility and calmness, I could find my happiness. Now I am more aware of this, and I know the value of tranquility. I now give myself permission to enter into these states and expand them inside me without fear and anxiety. With practice, I have learned to completely change and transcend my limited states of consciousness. We can all do this—transform ourselves from the inside out—by transcending our own ego.

A thought has come to me recently that in life it is good to become a student of elevated states of consciousness. To always study and focus our attention on the nature of love, appreciation, wisdom, tranquility, peace, creativity, beauty, and joy. When we do this, we fill ourselves up with these things naturally. When we think about, talk about, and study love, it is impossible for this state of consciousness to not fill us inwardly.

Transcendence is more like salvation or renewal of the mind in Christian terms. You go deep within yourself, and you allow that which is not real to vanish and that which is real to come forth and fill your consciousness. It is a natural process that takes place in meditation. You become aware of your True Self. God-qualities are an integral part of your True Self. These qualities are Life, Love, Wisdom, Intelligence, Peace, Creativity, Beauty, and Joy. When you let your True Self unfold in your life, you express these qualities freely.

Ernest Holmes talks about these God-qualities in his book, *How to Change Your Life*. He says, that unless all of these qualities are experienced fully in your life, you need to become more aware of your unity with God. This is what purpose of the Love Field is—to liberate you from your illusionary self and qualities you've acquired and learned during your lifetime that are keeping you bonded to negative states of being. The nature of your soul is free, loving, nurturing, secure, confident, beautiful, peaceful, tranquil, and joyful. God is what you are. Your task is to focus your attention on who we truly are and let go of all that feels painful, fearful, discouraging, limited, and lacking. To transcend these states is a natural ability we possess because stepping into our True Essence is the goal of the evolution of this world.

—

I have people asking me a lot about what I feel during meditation, how long does it take to have a transcendental moment, or how fast can I get the answers to my questions. Some even ask how many times they should sit in meditation until God reveals Himself to them. These are all good questions, but they are asked by our ego. Only the ego needs to know when the miraculous thing will happen, or when that extraordinary experience where you commune with God will happen to you. There is no answer to these questions.

If you sit in meditation interested to feel a more elevated state of being, you will experience this communion, transcendence, and Love Field sooner or later. Things will reveal themselves at the right time. Our mission is to follow that voice within, which always guides us towards our divine path on this Earth. When God reveals Himself to us is not something we can control. We shouldn't even try to control it, as controlling life is a miserable job. We must surrender to the beauty of life and to the energy of love, freedom, and liberation. Focus your attention on these things and you will be very surprised when, how, and in what order God reveals Himself. Surrender is a necessary condition for any kind of unfoldment and manifestation.

CHAPTER 7

PRAYER

*"Every thought you have brings
either peace or war; either love or fear."*
– A Course in Miracles

*W*e started our practice with knowledge in Part I. From there, we established our intention, familiarized ourselves with the eternity of the present moment, embraced the ideas of awareness, and decided to contemplate what true realization means. In the practice part of this book, we started with the practice of relaxation and then we stepped into the practice of meditation. All these steps are necessary to move into the practice of prayer. Meditation is a steppingstone towards prayer.

We've been raised through many religious traditions to think about prayer as a practice of asking God to fulfill our needs. When we are in a position of needing something—be it luck, health, money or a romantic relationship—we seek advice from spiritual mentors in our lives. And often, they say to us, "Why don't you pray for it?" In this regard, prayer has been portrayed as something to turn to when we are in a position of lack; we go with our neediness to the Divinity of the Universe to ask for It, God, to fill our need.

No wonder many of our prayers are not being answered or fulfilled. The reason is not that God doesn't want to support us, but it rather our energy when we pray is blocking the blessings we are meant to receive. Many of us live thinking God has no idea what we need and want. Therefore, we go into prayer to somehow bring to His awareness what we are lacking. I lived almost my entire life thinking God has no time for me and was not very aware of my life conditions or my problems.

The truth is that God knows what we need even before we know what we need, and He always knows what is going on with us. If you are a parent, aren't you 24/7 aware of the well-being of your child? Most people don't go for hours, days, weeks, years and not know what's going on with their child because they had children to be a source of love and support for them, tending to their needs with care.

I believe God has given us the possibility of having children not only for the evolution of our species but also for us to understand the nature of our Divine Source through Love. I remember when I got pregnant, a friend of mine said, "I am so happy for you. Now you will find out what true love is." I didn't understand her at that time, but I understand her now after experiencing motherhood. This is the love of God for us—true love: the absolute, unconditional, and nurturing energy that only He can have towards his creation.

In prayer, we do not need to ask for our needs, we just need to trust that God knows everything we need and open to receive. We need to go into prayer with our hearts full of love and open ourselves to a communion with our Heavenly Father.

THE ANATOMY OF PRAYER

Recently, I have changed my perception about prayer. I lived for a long time thinking that prayer is where I go to just seek relief, talk to God, and tell Him how my life is going, as though He had no idea about it. What I have come to understand is that prayer is not just a simple conversation with God. Prayer is a process—a process where we open ourselves to the divinity within us, where we unite ourselves with our Divine Source.

Prayer is a magnificent process. As *A Course in Miracles* describes, the Son and the Father become one when we pray. In prayer, we shift our energy so much so that all which is lacking in our life is automatically filled up once again. The nature of our divinity is never-ending abundance, so when we step into our true nature, as we do in prayer, everything is re-established. The divinity in us is recognized, and this divinity reunited with its Source. In prayer, we can talk to God, we can share with him our thoughts and feelings, but first we need to understand that God is not someone "out there," as we discussed in the earlier chapters. God is within us—always present, always available, and always loving and nurturing.

What happens in true prayer is we open the gates of our consciousness to receive all that has always been ours: the wisdom, the love, the beauty, the gratitude, the peace, the creativity, the joy. We open ourselves to receive the understanding of our True Nature. As you progress on your spiritual path towards all that you are seeking, you will realize that it is absurd to want abundance, or to want health, or to want money, or to want love. It is absurd because we are the source of all these things. We are not separate from it, as our ego has been telling us.

Through prayer, we embrace and step into our divinity. That is why we find relief from our problems; that's why we find peace and tranquility; that's why we become satisfied

103

with life; and that's why we start loving life more—because we are love itself. Inside us there is an eternal well of love, health, peace, fulfillment, and abundance.

We need to stop looking for all these things outside of ourselves. I see these days all sorts of people trying to teach how to have more abundance, how to have more peace, how to find love. They are missing the entire point. A human being is a spiritual being having a human experience. A spiritual being coming from its Source is already the source of everything. The source of us all is the essence from which everything comes in the physical realm and in the spiritual realm—through God. There is really no need to go search for anything anywhere else.

Inside of us is that from which everything is made. We are the source of abundance. We do not need to look for money or look for ways to get money or any physical manifestation. Inside of us exists that which can manifest all these things. The idea is to step into this True Nature of ours and stop walking around living like we lack this and this, thinking there's so much that we "need" in life.

Prayer can help us understand who we are and step into the Divinity within us. We need to stop acting like depleted individuals and start acting like children of the Most High God, knowing we are always loved, always fulfilled with everything we need, always at peace, and never forgotten. When we start living from that place, our material world will be a manifestation of the true abundance that is within us all. This is not a lesson on abundance, but it is a lesson on understanding and stepping into our True Nature.

So first, we need to grasp who we truly are. With this understanding, we can step into prayer. When we go into prayer knowing that our Heavenly Father is not in a Heaven somewhere outside of ourselves but exists in the Heaven within us, our hearts start opening so much. The amount of unconditional love we feel is beyond what our egotistic mind can comprehend. This is where we reach the Love Field: the place of true love—the place of true union between ourselves and God.

More than a year ago, before I understood the true nature of prayer, I went to see the priest of the church I was visiting on Sundays. I wanted to ask him about my prayer practice. Until that point, I did not have a consistent practice, and I kept feeling the call to create a structure for my practice. When I went to meet Father George, I told him that I felt the need to sit every day in prayer and thought I should structure the time I engage in this practice. I asked his guidance on what to say, what to prayer for, and advice on how this process might go.

First, Father George told me that I was being blessed because I had this urge to go sit in prayer. He said that God was calling me to go spend time with Him. At the time, I understood this as I should go somewhere to visit God more often.

I replied, "Okay, being blessed feels really good. But how do I do the whole practice? What is the structure I need to follow?"

Father George looked at me and said, "Prayer does not have a structure. Your mind wants to structure it because it wants to control it. Prayer is a surrendering practice. It's like going and spending time with someone you love. When you go spend time with someone you love, you don't want to force things or control things, you just want to be in their presence."

This answer was a real novelty for me. First, I thought Father George was giving me a lesson about love. I felt blessed again to have his insight about that. But then, because I had gotten so used to my thinking that this practice needs to be controlled, as many of us are, I had believed I needed to know what to do exactly. Like in yoga, you do this pose and then that pose, and it's supposed to be a flow, but you are just controlling the entire thing with your egotistic mind. Well, flow in prayer is the nature of prayer. You cannot be in prayer and not be in flow, so controlling it just gets us out of prayer.

After I visited Father George, that evening I got myself a candle, sat down in a quiet room, and closed my eyes intending to pray. My first words were, "Hello Father!" The minute I said those words, I was so surprised about what started to happen. My entire body started to be filled with this nurturing, loving energy—this is how I rationalize what happened. Maybe there are better words to describe it, but these are the ones that can say it right now.

The feeling was very, very different from anything I had ever felt up until that moment. It felt like the entire Universe was waiting for me to do this. I remember thinking, "How can two words trigger something so powerful?" Well, prayer is powerful!

You are basically communing with the most powerful force in the Universe. God is always in us, but we are so lost

106

in our egotistic mind that we completely live in total amnesia of this power within us. The thought seems so crazy that we can be totally emerged in a world where we walk around as some illusionary versions of ourselves, but it's true.

These feelings that come through prayer are possible because of belief. My experience in prayer happened because of my belief in the power of my Heavenly Father. The fact that we live amnesic of who we truly are, being completely forgetful of the God within us, is also possible because of the power of belief: our belief that such a world can exist, a world where God is absent from ourselves and everything else.

I made a habit of sitting in prayer every evening. At the beginning, I had no clue what to expect or say, but that was good. I was used to asking God for things. Slowly, I have let go of that practice. I remember having nights where I would just light the candle, sit for 2 minutes, blow it out, and be done. I also remember evenings where the resistance and entire daily baggage of pain and suffering melted in front of that candle. There were nights when the minute I said, "Hello Father," in an instant, an ocean of love would pour abundantly over my mind, my soul, and my heart. I would feel completely at peace, surrendered, and reassured after a day of turbulence. So, this is how I started to practice true prayer. This is how I started to open myself to receive what was already mine.

In prayer, you open yourself to a greater power. You acknowledge that there is something more powerful than what your mind can do and understand. You open your consciousness to God.

If you are feeling lack, like something is missing in your life, it is also a good time to go into prayer. In prayer, you can allow all that is missing to be filled. But you need to first understand that it needs to be filled within your consciousness, and then will it be manifested in the material world.

What is in your consciousness manifests in your outer world. If you want to be free, to find healing, to find love and joy, then you need to fill your consciousness with those feelings, you need to fill your consciousness with God. You can do this in prayer.

In prayer, the veil of illusion subsides because you have set an intention to commune with God. *A Course in Miracles* states the reality of ourselves and of this world is God, and everything else is an illusion created by the mind. We see negative aspects of life because our vision is distorted by illusions. The text also says that when you train your mind to see and look for God, you start remembering him, because His awareness is written on your consciousness. And because God is within us, this incredible creative power is also within us.

The creative power within is the reason we can even create a world that believes in the absence of God. Scarcity and poverty of any kind is not actually something that exists; it is more a mental construct in our consciousness. The nature of God is abundant and full of love, anything else outside this idea is an illusionary fact.

As God's creation, it is absurd to declare that we are poor, ill, or lacking anything. The outside world can reflect these illusionary states because we have chosen to believe in them, so we create them by the power of our conscious creation. How about we step into our True Nature, into the

God within us? We can go into prayer every day and train our old consciousness that believed in lack and limitation to embrace and remember the God within us.

How about we start believing that in us exists an unlimited source of love? We don't need to ask others to give love to us—we are love itself, looking to pour into everything, looking to express itself in everything, and expand itself in unlimited ways.

If you haven't been praying until now, I encourage you to start sitting in your quiet chamber. Your Creator is calling you by bringing this book into your hands. If you've been practicing prayer, just as I did for many years, by demanding the attention of God, then you might reconsider the way you approach your practice. In prayer, your consciousness is going to change and stay open to God. You cannot predict the ways in which the Divine will fill your mind and will change your energy. You for sure will be surprised.

YOU

I have spent a lot of time in my life being afraid to live. Fearful living can cause tremendous psychological and spiritual pain because we are out of alignment with who we truly are. I consider one of the most important tasks in my life to be finding ways to break free from fear. Due to the existence of our ego, we experience fear almost daily.

I first read in *A Course In Miracles* that each thought expresses either fear or love, either war or peace. I started to understand that I have a choice. I can choose fear, or I can choose love. I'd been choosing fear a lot because of my unconscious thoughts and programed thinking patterns. The reason that I wrote this book is to help others overcome and transform this fear.

At the core of who we are is our Divine Nature. Understanding and stepping into our Divine Nature automatically removes all fear-based thoughts and patterns. To truly step into your authentic Self, you need to work within yourself to move beyond your ego. Otherwise, life will do the work on you, without your consent.

The goal and purpose of life is awakening to your spiritual nature, but life will throw you into situations and circumstances where you will feel pushed. You might even want to run away and leave. But the purpose of these challenges is to offer an opportunity for you to transform parts of yourself that are keeping you bonded to the illusionary way of thinking, which is that you are anything else but a child of God. If we choose not to see the truth and not to listen to that voice within us, life will throw more experiences our way until we acknowledge God and surrender to Him. Life manifests for our best interest. We might not understand this at times, but it does.

In prayer, our egotistic self begins to die slowly. We start moving our attention away from the illusions of this world to what is True, Authentic, and Real. Racing around and living our lives hectically without grasping who we truly are inside gives birth to a lot of anxiety, depression, and frustration. To overcome these feelings, we need to step into our Divinity: search for it, study it, pay attention to it, and try to understand it. Only by fully focusing our attention on our

Divinity can we enter it and re-become it. Our Divinity has all the answers, all the solutions.

Recently, I went to get my nails done, and my nail technician confessed that she is pregnant with her fourth child. My instant thought sounded like this, "What's wrong with this woman? How can she put herself into this kind of situation? She probably does not want to work anymore and wants to stay home. After all, her job probably doesn't fulfill her very much." Well, I'm not going to discuss how wrong these thoughts are right now. The point is that I caught myself being judgmental first and then thinking illusionary thoughts second. I saw this woman just an individual who wants to sabotage her destiny by having so many children to care for. I did not look at her as a Divine being, as a child of God with a divine purpose; I looked at her as someone of very low value just because she is a nail technician.

We all do this kind of thinking daily no matter how hard we try to stay sane. The media and the societal conditioning are actually training us to look at each other based on our accomplishments, our jobs, our statuses, and our net worth. In this crazy ride to find meaning, we end up depressed, afraid, and anxious, because we are entangled in thought processes and energy field that is depleting us constantly through its illusions and untruths.

We are already accomplished as Divine Beings; we don't need to succeed at something as proof of our worth or as proof that we are deserving of love and appreciation. We have created a very false social value system. Instead of living our lives as though we must prove something for our family and friends to look up to us or give us approval, we can do things because we want to explore our creativity, expand our consciousness, multiply our energy, and spread it into the cosmos. These should be the reasons we do anything in life.

Unfortunately, because we are raised to focus on making money so we can survive in this world, we miss out on living at all. We are focusing our energy on getting what is absent from a place of absence, which never works. It's time to remember we can manifest from a place of abundance and plenty.

In prayer, our consciousness shifts. We give the control of our life, which we are holding onto so tightly, to Someone greater than our ego mind. Our ego wants to control, but our soul will always want to surrender to its Source. We surrender the limitations of our egotistic self and illusionary ways of thinking into the hands of our Divine Source. In this process of surrendering, our personality changes, our ego takes a back seat, and the Christ within us rises and takes stand.

If you would like to test yourself and your faith, start doing something new—a big project in your personal or professional life. Notice what happens inside you. Are you filled with a tremendous amount of anxiety, which makes you sleep poorly? Are you projecting negative expectations of the outcome? Are you feeling completely out of balance because you are afraid that you will not know what to do? These are all signs of not trusting life, of not trusting you, of not trusting God and of not knowing who you truly are. Does that mean you should consider yourself very out of Divine order? Absolutely not. Your life is in perfect Divine order always, no matter what's going on. And I can give you proof.

Writing this book, I was surprised because I realized that everything coming through was not specifically my words. The entire process was more like a channeling process. I was the faucet, God is the water, and this book is the container of water.

I made a pledge to write every day. Well, the thing is, I did not feel good every day and didn't always feel like writing. I learned that no matter how tired, exhausted, depleted, or anxious I felt, I could still be the faucet. The words that poured down on these sheets of paper amazed me because, as I said, these are technically not my mind's words. God can pour through me no matter how I feel and in whatever kind of illusionary state I am in.

This is the answer to the question above about if it's possible to be out of Divine order. No! No matter how far away we feel from God, God is never far away. He is within us, always present, always available to pour through us and into our lives.

Imagine now how the Divinity in you is present even when you feel depressed and anxious, and left out. Now you realize that you are actually never left out. The most powerful force in the Universe is always with you, is always in you, and always loves you. He is proud of you, very fond of you, and has so much appreciation for you. That's why when we step into prayer and we acknowledge our relationship and our origin in the Divinity of the Universe, our consciousness becomes filled with love, gratitude, beauty, creativity, joy, and freedom. We are always filled with those things, we were just looking and acknowledging the other ways.

Religious Science explains there is a creative force in each individual, and this creative force is what helps each and every one of us to create our lives, our destinies. The reason that some use this creative force to create more love, more beauty, more freedom, and more joy is because they decide to believe in these things. Those who use this creative force within to create lives filled with despair, fear, anxiety, and scarcity are holding onto opposite beliefs, which are illusions. This creative force is the creative force of God.

As many spiritual texts state, the Son has been created like the Father. Christ was not just in Jesus; we all have the Christ within us. It comes down to the choice we choose to make every day. We can wake up and sit in our quiet chamber of our mind and let the God within us rise and lead the way, helping us in letting our personality express itself in loving and meaningful ways. Or we can wake up and forget again about God and about ourselves and let anxiety and fear fill our hearts for another day in the calendar.

A powerful prayer that changed my life is one I wrote some time ago. It is called the Prayer for the Higher Self. I am including it here for you to pray, so that it can change your life the way it did mine.

Dear God,
I stepped into despair again,
I have forgotten You again.
I tried to live without You every day.
My life feels like a weight that makes my body age,

But I no longer want to walk in pain.
Today, I let You lead me where You want me go.
My heart is open and my soul awaiting,
For the recognition of Its True Identity.
I let You, God, write Your presence on my consciousness.
I let You, God, lift my life into the gifts of Heaven.
May I remember once again Your love, Your freedom,
    and Your goodness.

May I embody You in every word I say;
May I embody You in every step I take;
May I embody You in every thought I think;
May I embody You in every breath I take.

Deliver me from all my old ways,
So I can step into the loving nature of Your presence.
Amen.

In her book *Illuminata*, Marianne Williamson offers a great number of prayers that can also help you get started with your prayer practice or assist you in elevating your existing practice. I found this book incredibly powerful and useful when I started my prayer practice, and I continue to refer to it every now and then. Each time, I am transformed by the words Marianne has used to create her prayers.

I have realized over the years that any time I step away from walking on my path towards my Divine purpose, exhaustion, anxiety, frustration, or depression starts emerging into my consciousness. Recently, I heard a spiritual teacher say something meaningful about exhaustion. People these days are not tired and exhausted because they have so much to do or they are not resting properly. It is because their to-do lists and their lives are filled with things that are not meaningful to them, that are not meaningful to their true self. It was an eye-opener for me. As a toddler mom, my role as a parent is very meaningful to me, but is not all that there is in my life. The first months, even year, of your child's life can be tiring, putting aside all the other things that are meaningful and fill you up energetically and spiritually.

All the negativity in our lives is a message, an indicator that we are not walking on our Divine path; we are not being our true self; we are not letting God step into our conscious-ness and make our lives be divinely created.

Here is a very simple but a very powerful prayer that you can use anytime:

God, please rise within my soul and make me whole again.

GOD

Ernest Holmes teaches in his book *How to Change Your Life* that God is what we are and our life is the life of God within us. Many have become accustomed to talking to God like He is somewhere out there, separate from us. Even in prayer, there can be a tendency to speak to God like He's not within us.

During the meditation that inspired me to write this book, where I encountered the Love Field, I started to better understand the nature of God as Love. I don't differentiate

Love from God because I think God is Love and love encompasses everything of Divine nature. We all constantly wish each other love and happiness, as though we truly know what they mean.

We try and live our lives thinking we know what Love is. We gauge if we have it or if we don't have enough. But how does love expresses itself? What is reality when love is present? I have come to understand that Love is a blessing.

Finding out that Love is always present within you is a blessing. You can start looking at imperfections, and things that bothered you before don't bother you anymore. This vision is a blessing. This reality is a sign that in your heart Love started to fill you up.

Treating ourselves with Love and treating others lovingly is a major sign that you are stepping into your Divine nature. Many times, we choose to withhold love towards others and ourselves because we have learned that we can be mistreated, hurt, and betrayed. But no amount of hurt can make what's inside you, Love, be less than what is. No amount of betrayal can change your True Nature. And no amount of pain and suffering can make you anything else than a sacred creation of God.

During our childhoods, we learned to be afraid, to close ourselves, and not let what is inside us express itself because it got treated unfairly; people around us have used our openness, our vulnerability, and our kindness as a weapon against us in times of despair. I clearly remember, in the society that I grew up, people who were kind and compassionate were considered people that others would take advantage of. The

117

saying, "You need to be smart and not kind," was going around and filling up people's subconscious at every corner.

I grew up rigid of the notions of kindness and compassion. I was brought to believe that these are traits of the weak. No wonder, even today, I still catch myself in the relationship with my husband, withholding this part of me that wants to share love and kindness, totally open to giving and receiving. I have built an armor around me to protect myself from getting hurt. This is a practice I started to build from the age of 12, and continued sustain through romantic relationships in my 20's that failed one after another.

Today I am a devoted student of Love. I study it. I make it a priority in my life. I am continuing to learn the nature of who I am is kind, compassionate, loving, patient, nurturing and giving. Because this is the nature of God.

I also decided to let these qualities inside me develop and awaken because the rigidity I lived with ruined all my dreams of being soft and open. The most surprising thing I realized was that my true freedom came from me accepting and nurturing this part of myself. This part which I thought was nonexistent that I mostly feared and stayed away from, both consciously and unconsciously.

Love is patient. Love is kind. Love is compassionate. Love never hurts. Love always nurtures. Love accepts and surrenders. Love forgives, love shares and never withholds. Love makes you free and untethered.

After I gave birth to my daughter, I found myself in a world of despair. I didn't know what was going on with my body, with my mind, and with my soul. I felt completely left out, falling into a deep ocean of fear and anxiety. Now that I

118

am on the other side of it, I can see clearly that I wasn't able to love myself. I didn't know how. I was trying, but I had a very hard time accepting my new life as a mother.

Because I had no idea how to navigate the transition, I wasn't a very pleasant presence for others. I could not extend something that I was not able to give myself first. It is impossible to love others when you feel depleted yourself. But despite the chaos and the horrific world within my mind at the time, someone has always been there reassuring me that this too shall pass. I couldn't love myself, but God loved me.

Through this painful energy of this experience, I transformed and awakened better parts of myself through the Love of God. My ego thought every day during that time that I was going to die, I would not make it, that life was too hard. Panic attacks were present morning, day, and night for weeks.

Life is different now. As I look back, I would not change a thing. This experience transformed parts of me that were long overdue to change. Looking at all the crises and struggles of my soul, I find a common thread. The thread is a constant longing for security, for acceptance, for fulfillment, and for love.

No matter how many illusions I have believed in until now, the truth is that only God can fill up the longing and lift me up from despair. At times, I thought maybe I need my family to live closer to me, maybe I need a more loving partner, maybe I need more money or more success in my career, but these thoughts were masking the true longing for God.

For me, prayer is the practice when I completely surrender. It is when I completely acknowledge my heritage, my origin, my Divine nature. It is where I get a glimpse of where my real home is. God is our true destination, our true home. There is no place on this Earth, in this Universe, in our mind, or in our hearts that fulfills us, accepts us, nurtures us, and loves us as much as the presence of our Heavenly Father.

God is not something out there. He is the energy in you, the Christ within. If you decide to pray often, this part of yourself will take space within you. He will fill you up and awaken you, and you will start loving yourself. You will start seeing others with loving eyes. You will start to finally and truly love life and all that encompasses it.

Here's a prayer for you that I use often:

God, please rise where You already abide.
I surrender myself to You, I surrender my life to You.
Enter into my mind, take space within my heart and fill
*   my soul with You.*
My body is Your temple, my life is Your creation.
Lead me into love and goodness and eternity.
God, I give myself to You.

OPENING THE GATES OF CONSCIOUSNESS

A daily prayer changes and reshapes who you are. In prayer, you awaken. In prayer, you find out the truth of who you are. In prayer, you find what true surrender means.

In prayer, we are not praying to God; we are opening the gates of our consciousness for God to enter. Our consciousness has been torn by the illusions of this world and it needs redirection. Redirecting towards the realization that we are already Divine spiritual beings. We remember that God already lives within us, in our consciousness, no matter how many illusions we believe in.

The healing of the mind and the healing of the soul is only necessary when we have become so entangled with life's untruthful reality – when we are trying to build our lives rather than letting God shape us from within. In the Bible, verse Romans 12:2 Phillips reads, "Let God remold your mind from within and not let this world squeeze you into its own mold." In prayer, we let God remold us from within, we step into our divinity and let it reshape us, reconstruct us, and rebuild us.

It is very easy to want stuff, no matter what area we are talking about, be it relationships, career, money, health and even spirituality. We are always bombarded with sources of desires. Then we find ourselves running around, trying to create this ideal life all by ourselves. Yet we become stressed, worried, and depleted. Only then do we realize that we need to reconsider what we are doing and reconnect with God.

My relationship with anxiety and exhaustion is a great example of what happens when you stray away from your God-given life. Many times, I found myself waking up at 4am and having all these ideas about what to do with my life, as if there was a contest for who is building the best life and I was competing. I would be so excited for a little over 15 minutes, and then I would go online or start reading so I could start building this life and transforming all these ideas into reality. Then after 30 minutes, a huge wave of anxiety and exhaustion would come over me. I would start doubting, and question how in the world I would bring all these ideas to life. The problem was not the ideas; it was my overall intention and focus on how my life should unfold.

In the midst of my struggle with anxiety, my only option was to stop and relax. If I continued with my ideas and plans, my overall well-being would be at stake. I even remember one day when I developed symptoms of a urinary tract infection after a very stressful day filled with anxiety. I was very aware of my body, and therefore I was stunned to see the manifestation of its wisdom so instantaneously.

In the process of my awakening, including this stopping and backing off, I concluded that I needed to stop wanting, I needed to stop wanting to do things so I can feel that I am alive. I saw that my life is not my project—my inner world is my project. My task is not to figure out what to do, my task is to find the truth of who I am.

Starting to move towards this new path for me meant accepting that a lot of healing needed take place. I thought if I ate healthy, then I was physically healthy. If I was doing yoga and meditation for almost a decade, then my mind and my soul were healthy. Yet even eating well and exercising, I was still suffering from weight gain. I was still prone to become anxious, and it happened almost every other day.

Finally, I accepted the idea to embark on a journey of complete healing: healing my body, healing my mind, and healing my soul. I never thought I needed to be healed, I always thought I was okay, even in the midst of my crises. I knew that I needed to transform, but this transformation for me then meant like I was living with this color purple, and

I had to change to live with color green. Transformation for me never meant to heal.

Another reason I didn't understand that I needed healing was lack of compassion towards myself. I was preoccupied with how I should become more compassionate towards others, but to become compassionate towards myself always felt like an unnecessary task. No wonder I felt so anxious and exhausted for so long!

Healing for me started in prayer. My openness to new ways of understanding God and life has brought into my consciousness the reality of how depleted, hurt, and in desperate need of healing I was. Prayer was my starting point.

We cannot transform or step into something different when we are in denial or unconscious of our current state of being. I thought I was very aware of myself, of my thoughts, of my programming; but deep down, I was swimming into such a deep ocean of pain that I had to completely stop and start focusing on how to heal that first. We have doctors for everything, but to heal our hurt and pain, there is no one out there more suitable than the Doctor within us. In prayer, I started to go to the Doctor so I could heal, I am still seeing Him.

When we start to commune with our Divine source in prayer, healing and transformation start immediately. The energy of God has the highest frequency there is. Pain and hurt cause very low frequency energies. The high vibration of God literally is lifting your entire being into the highest vibrational energy.

When I started to pray, I had no idea what I was doing or how to do it. I just started most of time in my mind with the words, "God, please enter into my life and make all things right." I had no idea how God would enter my life and my mind, I just stayed open and accepted whatever was coming.

So here is some guidance. I recommend you start with a morning and evening transformational prayer. By having a morning and an evening practice, transformation and healing is inevitable. During both the morning and evening, when you sit in the quiet chamber of your mind, say these prayers to start the process of your communion.

Morning Prayer

Dear God,
Today is a new day,
Today I let You lead the way,
Today I allow myself to be filled with You,
Today I let life unfold by Your grace,
Today I choose to see the goodness of my life experience.
Your breath fills my heart with joy and freedom
and eternity.
May I stay centered into the presence of Your
eternal love,
May I embrace in every thought I have . . . the nature
of Your Mind.
Today I allow the peace of Your divinity to abide
within me and direct my footsteps.
I let You rise and take space within me, God,
I let You, God, expand Your energy within my soul,
I let You, God, be the authority of my destiny.
I step into Your grace today,
I step into Your joy today,

I step into Your freedom,
I step into Your beauty,
I step into Your peace and love.
Keep me in Your loving chamber.
Do not allow the wickedness of this world to pull me in
*   its directions.*
But instead, use me and my life to create the Heaven
*   that You are.*
I let myself immerse into Your presence.
Do through me what You would want me do.
Bless everything I touch and say.
Let everything that comes out of me reveal Your pure
*   and loving Presence.*
Dear God, fill me today and every day with You.
Amen.

Evening Prayer

Dear God,
I surrender to You this day now over
My heart feels heavy, and my soul confused
Take me and clean the heaviness and the confusion.
Remind my soul of its True Nature.
Wash it in goodness and in love and in redemption.
Release my heart from all the burdens.
Enter my mind and dissipate all illusions of pain
*   and suffering.*
Remind me, God, again Who lives within me and
*   Whose life I am living.*

I let the memories of my past and the worries for
    my future
be burned, transformed, and resurrected into the fire of
    Your Truth.
I surrender to Your presence and allow myself to
    be immersed into the restful sleep that You would
    have me be.
I let Your powerful divine love clean me, nourish me,
    and restore me.
During this night, transform my soul and liberate
    my mind.
I recognize, dear God, Your Power and Your
    Perfect Love,
I let You infuse me with their essence.
Help me to see the Truth of who I am and Who You are
    so I can live my life in freedom, joy, and peace.
Amen.

I personally recite prayers throughout the day. Reciting them changes my energy, and the prayers change me with every single day. Feel free to say them as often as you like, whenever you feel called.

May this chapter on prayer illuminate you and awaken you to step into a practice of true prayer, which will heal you, liberate you, transform you and your life, and bring you into the hands of Peace, Love, and Freedom.

CHAPTER 8

NURTURING THE RELATIONSHIP

"There is nowhere you need go to find God, for God is within you. There is no one you need ask if you are good enough, for He has already established He is exceedingly well pleased."
– Marianne Williamson

*N*ow that you started to sit in meditation and prayer and are becoming familiar with your eternal Self, it is time to talk about how your relationship with the Divine gets nurtured every day. It is in your highest and best interest to make the nurturing of your relationship with God a daily practice. You see, your Divine Source is already whole and complete and doesn't need attention or love. It is you who is prone to developing a strong ego that needs guidance and re-connection every day to stay centered into your Highest Self.

A Course in Miracles teaches that we can practice spiritual principles that can help us remember God, meaning become aware of our Divinity. Meditation and prayer are two pivotal practices that can keep us centered in our Sacred Self.

TIME

I saw a hypnotherapist once and did some hypnotherapy in a difficult moment of my life. In one of my sessions, the therapist took me back to the early years of my life. As incredible as it sounds, she also took me all the way back to the time when I was in my mother's womb, just prior to the moment of my conception. I later experienced and re-membered those moments of my existence in several guided meditations taught by a spiritual teacher that I follow. If you have ever had the experience to do this, you will know how powerful and revealing it is.

This practice helps you remember the eternity and the nature of your soul and who you were truly prior to the moment this world started to imprint itself onto you. The most remarkable thing about it all is that you have never changed. Your perception changed, but the joyful and free soul that decided to come and experience this life has never gone anywhere. You are still that Eternal Breath of Life within you.

Time, as we discussed earlier in the book, is a human mental construct; it does not really exist. Many times, we say that time heals everything and changes everything. It is actually not time doing that. It is just the false nature of what sheds away because it is nonexistent in reality. So when the mind forgets it, it ceases to exist.

Our mind forgets pain and suffering, frustration and stress, jealousy and betrayal, unless we decide to hold onto it and keep thinking about it intentionally so that we never forget. This is where the saying comes in: "I forgave, but I never forgot." It is not because of the severity of what happened, it is because we, with our own magnificent power of creation, decided to hold onto it and rebirth whatever has hurt us on a regular basis in our minds and hearts.

When it comes to devoting our time to remember who we are, there should be no day that goes by without us acknowledging the eternal nature of our soul, our sacred connection to our Creator. The reason for that is that our minds are always processing something, and if we let them run around like a monkey, it can get us into very dark places. This happens to us because it is very easy to believe in our ego. If we forget to claim the throne within us, which belongs to the Divinity within us, then guess who will grab the throne without even asking? Ego!

Our consciousness does not have a complete neutral state, where there is no God and there is no ego. There is always someone on the throne. By sitting in prayer every day, by reading and studying spiritual principles, by meditating and getting ourselves to be still and open to the God within us, we are less prone to having our egos step into a position of power within us and carry us all the way into despair and depression.

In recent months, I have realized why I felt so miserable during my life crises. I felt depleted, unloved, and unsupported because I was choosing to believe in scarcity—the scarcity of my soul, the scarcity of my life situation, and the scarcity of the people around me. You see, when we believe in scarcity, we are believing in lack and limitation. Scarcity means lack of love, joy, peace, and abundance; it also means the presence of hatred, violence, insecurity, jealousy, and burning hell (metaphorically speaking).

I literally believed that no one loved me, no one appreciated me, and that I was lost and no one cared about it. In those moments, the truth was that I was loved, I was appreciated, and I was cared for, not only by God, but by a lot of people around me too. I just couldn't see that because I believed the opposite of this, so it was impossible for me to see clearly what was going on. This is the reason that I pray and meditate every day—so I do not get into believing the illusions of this world and let them mold me to such a degree that I need an emergency divine intervention.

Every day, I nurture the connection to my Higher Self and to my Heavenly Father. Only in coming back to myself regularly keeps me awake and aware of the truth – the truth that I am always loved, cared for, appreciated, and valued, and nothing can change that, no illusion, no forgetful thought. As Marianne Williamson said, you do not need to ask if you are good enough, for your Heavenly Father has already established that He is exceedingly well pleased.

SPACE
The Love Field – God's Field

Nurturing the relationship with our Divine Source also means making the space in our lives for the Love Field. You must make room for this field in our consciousness to manifest into our reality. What does that mean, exactly, you might ask? Making space means letting go of everything that is contradictory to the nature of the divine, letting go of parts of ourselves and established behaviors that are constructing a life without God. Making space means also allowing yourself to be directed by something greater and trusting in the power of your Creator to guide you in building a life worthy of your divine destiny. Making space is waking up every day and starting to walk knowing that you are the child of the Most High God.

This life is so tricky if we let ourselves be guided by our egos. There is always something exciting, dopamine-triggering, or even terrifying to pay attention to. Our minds are easily distracted and influenced by the next big thing that comes up on our news feed. Sometimes we even become so passionate about other people's lives that we totally forget about our own.

In America, specifically, being famous is considered a remarkable success. People become obsessed with other people's lives, and in return, this turns out to make the fan and the star miserable. The fans live with a total lack of consideration for their own magnificent life and the stars becomes so isolated because they are not seen as a human being any longer but as some sort of deity, which creates such a huge space between them and others. No wonder famous people struggle so much. Imagine not being able to just go to Target or go to the store and buy bread, simple things that mean so much.

There are famous people in other countries too, but they can go to the public zoo with their kids without being chased by anyone. The problem is not the fame—the problem is our obsession with other people's lives. It is not okay to be so interested in someone's life. At times, I even catch myself saying, "Well, this person's life inspires me so much. It is normal to be interested, to know what her daily routine is, or what she thinks about veganism (for example)." But, it is not normal.

I think we become so obsessed with other people's lives because we are so inconsiderate of our own life. We think our life doesn't matter as much or that we are not as valuable as others. This makes us not pay attention to how we build our own lives and who we are while doing it. This is why social media thrives right now—we follow others because we don't know who we really are ourselves. We are lost in the opinions and the lives of others and end up with mental health deteriorating at a global level because of this simple and wrong perception of what our lives are. Plus, it's important to remember that social media does not reflect what is truly happening in people's lives.

I know a person who has been going through a very difficult health crisis, but in her social media posts, she was hiding it so well that no one knew what was truly going on. Everyone thought that she was doing so well and was so successful. Why are we doing this? We are all struggling with something at some point in our lives, why hide the struggle? The struggles of our lives do not mean we are weak, that we are doing things wrong, or that something is wrong with us. The struggles, as I've said previously, have a divine purpose. They are meant to grow us and transform us to such degrees that we wouldn't be able otherwise.

So, let's make space in our lives for authenticity first, admitting that we are struggling in one area or the other and there is nothing wrong with that. And let's start making space in our lives for the Truth that no matter how big of a struggle we face, the power within us is greater than any hardship there is. Let's let our Divine Nature fuel our life decisions, our behaviors, our energies, our careers, our relationships, and our minds.

Let's fill ourselves up with the idea that God is all we are. That we are always safe and protected, no matter the danger that our mind tries to articulate. That we are always loved and supported, no matter how much doubt our ego tries to impose on us. That we are a deep well of beauty, creativity, wisdom and joy, no matter how many destructive thoughts per day our mind would try to manufacture.

And slowly, after some time of doing all of this, you will wake up one morning and look out the window or go outside and be overwhelmed by the amount of appreciation and love you have for this life. You will realize that everything is a gift. You will see you have been so blessed that there is no amount of worldly understanding that can explain the elevated energy you feel. This is the nature of life. We are created thankful, grateful, full of love and appreciation for everything. The nature of God is our identity, everything else is just a distorted idea.

The way we make space for God in our lives is by understanding that the purpose of everything is love and harmony. This is the purpose in your relationships, in your career, in your daily activities, in your financial affairs, and all your personal areas. Because everything you will ever do is personal to you.

You will never be so separate from something that you could say it is not personal. You view and experience this world and yourself through your own filters, so everything is personal. You could never say, "Well, I will try and live from the God within me in the relationships with my family, but when I go to work tomorrow, I am going to be the same cold and distant person as yesterday."

You cannot do that because you are a whole being; different parts of yourself are always interconnected with each other. If you decide to live separate from God, you will live separate in all areas of your life, but if you decide to embrace who you truly are and live from that space, you will carry this in all areas of your life.

The purpose of everything is love and harmony. When you get up and go downstairs and you find dishes in the sink; when the weekend is here and you have nothing planned and no one to see; when you start to think your spouse doesn't care about your relationship, these situations are all instances where you can step back within yourself, within your consciousness, and decide to step into the Love Field in that moment. You can remember the identity of the One who is never displeased, who is never lost, who is never lonely, who is never worried, who is never afraid. Because this is who you are: you are always pleased, you are always reassured, you are always trustful, you are always loving, you are always kind, you are always fulfilled, and you are always whole. Never, ever forget that!

In every moment that you have forgotten again what your True Identity is, choose again. Choose to remember that none of the pain and frustration and sadness actually exist. They are your interpretations because you have viewed yourself, just for a brief moment, as someone separate from your Source. Make space. Make space every day within yourself, within your consciousness, and in your life to be and walk as someone so blessed and entitled to all the goodness there is, because you are worth it. You are the most marvelous creation of the most Powerful God there is.

ATTENTION

I would like to tell you that your attention is the most valuable asset you have. With your attention, you do everything in life. You are who you are because you are feeding your mind and your soul with certain information while you are awake; you are paying attention to certain things that eventually shape and create your life. In order to change yourself or your life, you need to change where you are investing your attention.

It starts with what kind of tea you drink in the morning and ends with your belief in how friendly the Universe is. In nurturing our relationship with our Divine Source, so that we can access the Love Field within us, we need to pay indestructible attention to it.

There are many ways to do this. Meditation is one way; prayer is another way. Also, studying spirituality, the nature of the Divine, metaphysics, science, and anything else you feel you resonate with will take you on the path to discover the Divinity of your soul and is a great idea to pursue.

By studying, you are paying attention and changing your beliefs. This is important because your beliefs then control your attention when you are unconscious. It is very important to build a belief system that has your best interests at heart because when you go unconscious, which is around 80% of the time, the ideas that are running your life are based on the Truth of who you are and not on what the world is trying to impose on you.

Right after I gave birth to my daughter, the global pandemic started. I found myself at home taking care of my child for long weeks and months. It became a very difficult time in my life and caused a new life crisis to emerge. I had a very hard time enjoying my life as a mother in the first year of my daughter's life. With the pandemic starting, I knew that my situation might not change anytime soon, as I had envisioned when I was pregnant. My reality was going to be different than the vision I had created in my mind. So, I had to surrender, which was a very hard thing to do.

My mental health deteriorated, and I found myself sinking into big waves of despair. This was the time that I started to read a lot. Before that, I read a good number of books per year, but at this time I was desperate to find some relief, so the speed at which I started reading to study the books was astonishing. It was like therapy for me. Then I noticed a pattern. I started to read more and more books about spirituality. I'd been studying spirituality for more than eight years by that time, but during those desperate moments, spiritual books felt like the greatest therapy I could find.

I even remember Marianne Williamson's book *A Return to Love*, which I have read multiple times prior to this time in my life, was a cure for my insomnia. Every evening I would grab my tea and my book, and I would sit on the sofa to read. It felt like I was in a soul hospital, and I was healing my mind and my heart of the depression I felt. And today, more than a year later, spiritual books remain my greatest therapy. I have healed myself and lifted myself out of a life crisis by studying the nature of God, by paying attention to that which is real and eternal, by learning about His power, His strength, and the Unlimited Source within my soul.

I recommend you start to direct your attention to the things that will strengthen your idea of who you truly are. Read books that are inspiring, encouraging, uplifting and empowering, because those books connect you with the energy of God. Be cautious and don't get seduced by the material out there that is produced based on an achieving mentality, which is very attractive to your ego. Pay attention to that which makes you believe that you do not need to buy another thing or do another thing in order to find yourself, to find freedom, to find relief, and to find love and joy. Pay attention to information that is affirming your God-like nature, affirming the tremendous Divine Power within you, through which you can change any life circumstance by transforming any depression into happiness, any fear into love, and any negative perspective into a positive one.

Stay away from anything that fuels fearful thoughts, which make you lean towards negative perceptions about life, people, and yourself. Refuse to become a part of conversations that do not serve the highest good of all. Use social media for the purpose to expand and share your truth; your truth will heal others including yourself.

Force yourself to let go of your ego—it is very clingy. Stay in prayer as long as you need to until you find the release from the ego. Ask the Christ within you to rise and help you build your life around God, around your Divine Identity. Every time you get lost in your egotistic views of the world, gently forgive everything and come back to God; drop every piece of shame and guilt and throw away all that feels constricting and retracting. Understand that in any given moment your soul should feel expanded, relaxed, and assured. If you feel the opposite of these, you have gone on the wrong road and you need to bring yourself back.

Take care of where your attention goes. Read, study, and make your life the territory where the energy of God expresses itself into this physical world. This way you will be sure that no matter how many illusionary forces come your way, you are staying centered in your True Identity.

CONSCIOUSNESS

Recently, I watched a video with Wayne Dyer, whose teachings and books have influenced my life tremendously. In this video, Wayne talked about the space within us. He made the analogy between us and a clay pot. If you would take a clay pot and smash it, there would be no clay pot because what made the clay pot was the clay and the space inside the pot. Wayne says that it is the same with us. Our body is the clay, but we cannot exist without this space within us. He called this space our consciousness or our soul. I call it the Life Force within us, the Divinity in us.

Consciousness is the force that drives life; it is that flow that is never hurried yet accomplishes everything.

Wayne Dyer also states that we are not doing anything but that we are being done. Your nails are growing without you doing anything, your heart is pumping without you doing anything. Life is doing everything for us. Then the question is why are we so insane and lose our minds worrying about every little thing? The answer is because we are very unaware of what this Life Force exactly is. We lack the knowledge and awareness of the truth of God.

When we open our consciousness to God, to our Divine Source, we also open ourselves to receive the awareness and the true knowledge about the nature of our Source. In this process, we also do not have to do anything mentally or physically, because the awareness and the knowledge come by themselves without us doing anything. Our goal is to have an intention to find out the truth, to get true vision, and the rest is done by the Life Force itself. This is a great lesson on how to relax and get in the flow—let go and let God.

In the same way our body is being kept alive, our consciousness can be directed to open and understand the Truth. The Love Field is a place within our consciousness. It is where we become everything, it is where life flows, and it is where we let God in because we see that we have gotten it all wrong until now. There is no pain and no suffering because love and freedom lie within us.

The Divine is the Source of the Love Field. When we become aware of the Divinity within us, we automatically embrace love and freedom because that is who we are. Everything that takes place—the Love Field, the awakening, the finding of freedom and joy—they all take place within our consciousness. We find God within our consciousness because that's where He has always been.

Our body is the temple of God. Ernest Holmes said:

"Your life is the life of God within you."

I will keep repeating this statement throughout the book because it is a very powerful one. It shifts your entire perception from an ego-originated one to a God-originated perception. Remember, every time you encounter any resistance, any pressure, any discord within you, it is a sign of you forgetting who you are. If we could just make the decision to relax and allow the Life Force within us to guide us, to

141

move us, to awaken us, to support us, and to love us, we would totally surrender to the flow of life and to the flow of God's energy within us. We would feel completely secure, protected, and loved.

I am, personally, still in the process of learning lessons about how to let go and let God. I catch myself entangled in anxiety and despair because I am making myself believe in the illusions around me. For the millionth time, I hit the fence of discord. But now I choose to awaken and forcefully let go of my limited perception.

Our minds are constantly being trained to believe in the ego, in the illusionary visions of this world. This is why we find ourselves hitting the wall of discord—we are investing our attention in untruthful ideas about ourselves and life. We fill our consciousness, many times, with anything but God. But as I said, the discord is your instrument for salvation, for redemption, and for awakening. Pay close attention to your feelings, to your intuition, and to the energy within you. And every time you feel yourself contracting instead of expanding, that is your sign to give up what you've been carrying in your consciousness—to let go and accept that you have lost true vision and understanding.

CHAPTER 9

COMMUNION

*"You're not looking to get this, you're looking to let
this. If you try to get it, you will repel it.
If you let it, you'll never be without it."*
– Michael Beckwith

*W*hat is true communion with our Divine Source? True communion comes from being and living from your authentic true Self. Your true Self is the God-essence within you. It is the Self that wants to forgive; it is the Self that wants to hug and comfort others; it is the Self that wants to give; it is the Self that seeks freedom; it is the Self that is free; it is the Self that loves, cares, and wants to expand itself into joyful life expressions. True communion with God does not involve a doing of something, but a being of something — a being of your Self.

Becoming one with God is a very freeing process, you feel like all the burdens have been lifted, physical, and spiritual. I lived most of my life totally unaware of my Divine Nature. I knew I had some sort of link with God, but I never experienced the powerful awareness of transformative moments until recently. Living every day feeling my Divine Source present in every second of it—in every thought, in every feeling, lifting me up every time I get lost in illusion—is a very, very nice place to be in. Life feels safe, reassuring, and is fulfilling from all angles. You start loving things you thought were unlovable; you start appreciating and seeing the value of things you thought were lacking value before.

As an example, I struggled for some time to love the house we live in. We live in a rental, but next year we are going to buy a house. I know that this is coming. So, I would spend my days focusing on what I dislike about our current place, saying that when we move our walls will be this color and our kitchen will be this way, totally disregarding any positive aspect of our current place. The thing is that living in a place you do not like very much affects your state of being tremendously.

But one morning, I opened my eyes, and I woke up with this incredible feeling of love for our current home. That was a big surprise! I wondered, "Where this is coming from?" I went to look at the carpet I disliked for such a long time and suddenly I didn't care—I liked it the way it was.

The way I can articulate this feeling of love and appreciation in my mind and my heart is like this, "I love our home because this is the only place where I feel at home, where I feel comfortable and loved, and it is where my family gathers after going places. This is home for all of us, and all this warmth is so nourishing to my soul. This is where my spirit lives, and between these walls there is a lot of love."

I can't say what exactly happened, but suddenly I started to see the truth about our current home. I realized that the color of the walls and the look of a carpet do not exist independently; they are connected to my home. A home is not just a house: a home is where our souls live. I share this example because this is what happens when you commune with God. You wake up and all of a sudden you love life in ways that you never thought possible.

LOVE

Given the fact that the core of who we are is Love, is God, is this high-vibrational Energy, any time we feel discord, we feel a deviation from love. A deviation from love means we have forgotten love in our mind, and we are filling our attitude with other things instead of love.

When we communion with the Divine, it is impossible to feel anything but love. Any time you have this expanding, nourishing, and beautiful feeling in your chest, you are in sync with your Creator. Any time you feel contracting, just "blah," or anything other than expanding, you are out of sync with love. This happens, but whenever we get sidetracked, a great habit to have is asking ourselves, "Where have I deviated from love and from God in this situation?"

True communion with God happens when we let our minds be filled with God, when we let our souls express themselves freely, when we let our bodies and every cell in them be filled with God's energy. When we let every emotion be fueled by love, this is communion. When we walk, we let God walk into every step. When we talk, we let God's words come through. When we hug someone or comfort someone, we let God hug them and comfort them. When we give, we let God give. And when we love, we love through God's love.

True communion is when we let our life be infiltrated and shaped by the Divinity of our being. This does not leave anything out; it includes everything—every aspect of our life and every relationship with every person in our life. This is the nature of the Love Field: abundant, filled with love, appreciation, gratitude, creativity, and joy.

A great way to strengthen your communion with the Divine is by using spiritual mind treatments. In the book *How to Change Your Life*, Ernest Holmes teaches how to use a spiritual mind treatment for personal use.

Here is a particular treatment that you can affirm as often as you would like:

Express Your Inner Perfection

I affirm the perfection of the Divine Pattern at the center of my being.
Realizing Its reality, I permit Its essence to flow through me, claiming it as my very own.
Believing in Its wholeness, perfection, and right action,
I know that everything in my experience conforms to Its nature.
Accepting Its peace, I am calm.
Accepting Its love, I am unified with life.
Believing in Its power, with childlike faith,
I accept the authority of Its action in my everyday affairs.
Today I declare the presence and activity of Spirit in that which I am
in my relationships with others and in my contacts with the world around me.

We've lived for too long entangled in our false ideas about who we are—that we are these human beings struggling to get ahead in life, chasing the freedom, chasing the peace, chasing the joy, and chasing the love. What absolute craziness it is to always carry all the Greatness of life within you and never know about it. What an incredible process of getting lost in an illusion that runs our lives to such a degree that it makes us completely clueless of the fact that the most Powerful Force in the Universe lives within us.

It took thousands of years to build up the memory of the illusion that we are separate from God. But also, it can take an instant second for the truth to blossom in our minds and hearts. We are free, we are love, and we are God. There is nowhere to go and nothing to do to find ourselves—to find our wholeness and fulfillment—because everything already lives deep within our soul.

Communion is not a process of meeting or getting together with God because you are not separate from God. Communion is a process of awakening, of self-realization of your True Identity. Within you breathes, walks, talks, and moves the most powerful force in the Universe. What else would you need? All the knowing, all the solutions, all the opportunities, all the wholeness, and all that you are looking for, you already are! Meditate on this; contemplate this daily. Ask God to rise within you in every second of the day, in every step you take, in any decision you make, with any people you meet, and in any thought you think.

APPRECIATION

Appreciation is the natural attitude of your soul. Any time you try and depreciate something or someone, offering a decrease in value, you are turning away from love to the illusion; you are covering your eyes with the veil again. What I mean by this is that in everything around you, there is God. In everything within you, there is God.

A Course in Miracles teaches that everything is infused with God and that the majority of us hold a perception so distorted from this truth that we see anything *but* God in all that is around us. Because of this distorted vision, we feel afraid and we see fear in everything. The opposite of fear is love; the opposite of fear is God. Since God is in everything, then everything has value. Everything is infused with light and abundance; everything has a divine purpose. Until we hold this vision, we are doing nothing but living in an illusion.

Living is a very enjoyable and fulfilling experience when you hold true vision. When you walk on the street and know that every human being walking along carries God within them, knowing that the weather, the energy between people, the street, and the cars are infused with God, how can you be afraid? There is nothing to fear when you understand Who walks within you, behind you, in front of you. Who holds the space above you and below you is the One who created you; the One who loves you because you are His most precious child; the One who holds the stars and the moon and the sun together for you; the One who breathes life into you; the One who never starts and never ends; the One who is only Love. You can never fear Love because Love never hurts, never destroys, never betrays, never leaves, and never transforms. Love is eternal and nourishing; Love is the universal purpose.

When you communion with God, when you let your consciousness be filled with God, you appreciate everything and you see the good in everything, not because you decided to think positively, but because you stepped into your True Nature. Within your soul sits an Energy that can transform your vision based on fear to a vision based on love. Let that Energy guide you, awaken you, and lift you up so you can see clearly how much Love, Goodness, Divinity lives within you.

GRATITUDE

If I would tell you that your normal and natural state of being is a state of gratitude, a state of thankfulness, wouldn't you start to give yourself permission to enjoy life more? To enjoy the simple things that you take for granted because your ego is convincing you daily of how mundane these things are?

Gratitude is the state of total bliss because Love can only give from Its abundant, never-ending supply. When we realize that everything we look at is infused with God, we start to become so grateful for all there is—for the air, for the food, for the people, for the Earth, for life itself. Everything on this Earth is here for a divine purpose—the chair that you sit in, the tree outside your window, the paint on the walls, the sound of your voice.

Being one with God is an everyday practice, and not only a practice but the purpose of life. A life where you breathe, you walk, you think, and you have your being infused with love, appreciation, gratitude, kindness, freedom, creativity, and joy.

Your belief in scarcity and not-enough-ness, your belief in your ego, has made you to live a life of fear and despair—a life filled with thoughts of destruction towards yourself, your world, and your brothers and sisters. *A Course in Miracles* teaches that the way you see others is the same way you see yourself. When you start seeing yourself as a divine creation of God, you extend this vision towards others, and the world becomes a place of peace, harmony, and love. It is your vision that is the root of all your problems. When you fix your vision, your world changes and fixes itself.

Communion is when you let go of your belief in ego and you accept and embrace your identity in God. Your subconscious mind might be loaded with beliefs in destruction, death, and despair from a lifelong repetition of thoughts and experiences attracted by those thoughts which reassure your ego. But God has never left your consciousness, your body, your mind, or your soul, no matter how many generations of people have come and left this physical world. Your Divine Source has always been there, has always loved you, and has always taken care of you.

You know this. You are reading this book; you are here right now. You have survived all your ego's insanity until now. This is proof that you can never be destroyed and nothing can harm you. No matter how many life crises you go through, no matter how many times you swim in despair, you are always whole, you are always saved, you are always loved, and you are always found because you are always and forever the child of the Most High God. You are eternal, and nothing and no one can change that. Remember this!

The Force within you, the Powerful Energy in you, can lift you up from anything, help you transcend everything, and change your life's direction to move towards Love. It has always been there. That's where the saying, "Everything that you need is within you," comes from. The God within you is the solution to all your problems.

You might still dream worldly ideas about how to fix yourself and your life, but no matter how long it takes you, you will still arrive to the one and only truth: you are a sacred being, a spiritual being, and within you abides the most Sacred Energy there is —the most Powerful Vibration that can move the mountains and light up the stars. You do not need to be fixed. You are already whole; you are already sacred. God has infused you with perfection—there is nothing to fix. You just need to come home, to come home to yourself and to your Heavenly Father, who abides within your sacred soul.

COMING HOME

The world we live in is hectic and chaotic. It is very easy to leave yourself and identify with other people's life conditions and situations. It is very easy to live in the past or the future. But coming home is also easy because home is a place that is easy to identify; it feels right, natural, and nurturing. Every time I sit in silence and close my eyes in meditation or prayer, I breathe relief that I don't have to go anywhere anymore. I don't need to try and live because Life is breathing Itself through me without a single effort from my part. This place of stillness, this place of nurturing peace, is always available. It is who we are. The author, Charles Barker, said that behind your problem there is something untroubled. There is something within that is never troubled or disturbed by anything. It is in your consciousness—the peace, the sanctuary, a place of complete untethering.

No matter who you are and what you do, you will never find God and His peace, joy, and freedom anywhere but within you. This is where God has placed Himself. He has given Himself to you; you don't need to look for Him in churches or in other places. He has placed Himself right within you so you can easily go within to find yourself and the peace of God.

153

Whenever you wind up believing your ego's insistence that you need to chase external life conditions to find what you are seeking, you will always get lost. That who seeks is God Himself in you; what calls you is God Himself in you. This part of yourself seeks to acknowledge Itself, to see Itself, to embrace Itself, to rejoice in Itself. The Oneness of God is crowded—crowded with freedom, joy, peace and love.

So make the decision to look in the mirror each day and look for God, see God, focus on God, and search for God. First you must find God within you. Only after you can see the God within you, will you be able to see Him in everyone and everything else. Make the decision to think about God, to think like God, because your mind is part of the mind of God. Make the decision to embody God every day; ask for guidance on how to do it in prayer. And have the courage to fall into the arms of your Heavenly Father with freedom and total trust, because that is the only place where you will find all that you are looking for.

In one of her prayers in the book, *Illuminata*, Marianne Williamson says:

> *"May I remember, dear God, that I live in Your mind*
> *and I belong in Your arms.*
> *For there I am healed, and there I am whole."*

The Love Field is a place of complete power, redemption from all hurt and pain, unshakable peace, and the great freedom which lies only within your soul. Your life is a stage where God is expressing Himself through you. You are an eternal being because an Eternal Energy has birthed you. Stay centered and breathe into the life within you, come home and let your mind be guided by the force of your Father, who never abandons you, who never forgets you, who never ever left you. You are always found; you are always home. You just need to open the eyes of your consciousness to see the brilliance of the One who lives within you—to see the goodness, the life, the joy, the love, the freedom that embodies you eternally, unattached to space and time.

Love is at the core of who you are. Life is the energy through which Love moves and expresses itself. Take your attention off your ego and let the grandiosity of who you are come through from the center of your being to express itself in everything you touch, say, think, and do. Let your sacredness blossom in the most beautiful life expression that ever existed. Let the God within you come forth and take space in your consciousness to transform all that is not of Himself.

CHAPTER 10

SPIRITUAL LIVING

*"The Word of God is written on your heart and his
awareness on your consciousness."*
– A Course in Miracles

L ife is a beautiful journey when we give up on fear and let our consciousness be filled with God. Believe it or not, we chose to be here. We chose to come here on Earth and express the Divinity within us. We came into this life to reveal and magnificently create another Divine expression into this physical dimension. Instead of living bonded by fear, anxiety, guilt, shame, despair, and depression, we have the choice to explore this journey through love, freedom, creativity, beauty, and compassion. Spiritual living does not mean going to church and sitting in prayer. Spiritual living is centralizing yourself into your own being, rooting yourself so deeply into the God within you that the ego is afraid to linger at your door.

A lot of people say that with experience comes wisdom. I say that through your decisions wisdom reveals itself. You are always a decision away from living in fear or living in the goodness of the Divine. You do not need time because, as we contemplated previously, time doesn't exist. You cannot awaken in an extended period of time; you awaken in a brief split-second. There are parts of you that transform over time that help you awaken, but you, yourself, your consciousness becomes aware of God in one single moment.

Your job is not to do anything in particular. Your job is to stay aware when you step away from your Divinity. Your job is to practice the awareness of your Divine Source every single day and to train your mind to always keep coming back to the ideas that support the Truth of who you are. Your job is to deposit into your subconscious mind the awareness of God because that's where the ego deposited itself during your childhood and adult life. When you deposit the awareness of God into your mind, the ego automatically disappears, because it cannot exist in the same place with your Divine Source.

COMPASSION

Compassion is a natural characteristic of a spiritual being. It is a trait that we already embrace within ourselves. The problem is that we might be lacking compassion towards ourselves and others because, once again, we have forgotten who we are. We forget compassion if we have no clue of our True Nature. Fear obscures a lot of our natural traits. Fear makes parts of ourselves seem invisible.

For example, when someone attacks you, let's say verbally in this case, your tendency is to protect yourself. You want to protect yourself because you are experiencing fear. In your effort to protect yourself from this fear, you might attack back. During this process, it rarely comes to your mind to contemplate why this person is attacking you.

Maybe they had a very rough day or their life is not going well. Taking the time to contemplate the other person's experience comes through compassion, which is a remedy for fear. This knowledge can help us shift and become more aware of how we act when we feel fear. Reflection makes us aware of how we step away from our True Nature by giving in to our ego.

Romantic relationships create the greatest space for learning to recognize our fear and stand up to our ego so that we do not react and respond from it. Just by knowing the signs of experiencing and reacting from a fear-based state helps us to transcend moments when we lose ourselves and come back to our compassionate nature.

Compassion is not something you have to force yourself into. If you find it hard and you feel that you need to force yourself to be compassionate towards yourself and others, it means you are not completely transcending your ego. You are still believing in what the ego is telling you and making you believe about yourself or other people.

Compassion is a consequence of Love. Love births compassion because the nature of Love is compassionate. Love heals, protects, supports, transcends, uplifts, empowers, and expands the Goodness in everything and everyone. By being the place where God abides, Love and compassion becomes your nature.

Deep within your soul, you are filled with Love for everything and everyone. From a desperate need, derived from an illusionary vision, you lose yourself in fear and attack that which you love. From now on, in every moment where you are about to attack something or someone, in your thoughts or your behaviors, pause for a moment and give your mind some space to contemplate this idea: what you are about to attack, you actually love and appreciate deeply, no matter what your current situation might be. Think about this and let the Spirit within guide you. Let your mind be picked up by God and let Him fill your thoughts with this Truth.

161

Compassion is an elevated state of being that an individual expresses when they understand the Truth about themselves and about God. Love is at the core of who you are, while compassion is the channel through which you extend your Love towards the ones that are hurting. This could be towards people who mistreat, hurt, or betray you.

You express compassion towards people, things, and a part of the world that you feel is dwelling in scarcity. You treat them with compassion because you know that at the core of who they are is what you are and there is no place where you begin, and they end.

ONENESS

There is really nothing to fear. Scarcity is an illusion; despair is an illusion; depression and anxiety are illusions; sickness is an illusion. Underneath your sickness is a perfect healthy spiritual being. Underneath the illusion is the Truth, which never ceases to exist. The Truth that we are one and the same. We are individualized expressions of God. At the core of our being sits the Source of everything, the Divine Force of the universe.

Next time you walk into a room, pay attention to what you feel when you look at everyone as expressions of the Divine. Your fears will disappear. Separation is what is causing anxiety, fear, and worry to exist. We might be walking around in different bodies, even though our bodies have the same anatomy, but we walk in the same Energy, we breathe the same Life. A great spiritual teacher once said that if we are separate, we would look at a flower and see different things.

We all see it as a flower because our minds are unified in one and the same mind—the mind of God. We feel the same feelings; we think the same things; we desire and seek the same things. But we are unique in the way we express ourselves because the nature of God is creative and abundant, so the gifts He has put in us are different. This creativity and abundance is for us to enjoy a Life expression of plentitude in love, joy, beauty, and freedom.

I walked into the gym today and what I saw was God everywhere. Still being conscious of it, I became aware of my tendency to reject looking people in their eyes. Our ego is guiding us to believe in our separation. The fear of looking and getting close to one another is not because we are afraid of being hurt by others, but we are afraid of the grandiosity that we might find in one another. We are afraid because we meet ourselves in the other, and the connection leads to seeing the God in ourselves and others—the ego finds this incredibly intimidating. This is why we feel shy and intimidated by the presence of others.

We are so rooted in our ego perception that our amnesia is directing us to make our belief in separation even stronger by judging one another and keeping the distance between us far apart. The truth is that no matter how big of an illusion we believe in, the truth underneath is bigger; God in our consciousness and ourselves is bigger than anything that the ego can construct. Deep within us, we love one another unconditionally; we are just walking around and pretending that we don't. We create ideals about how life and people should be, and based on them, we build our walls of separation in our consciousness.

163

Life is an opportunity to show and express the grandiosity of God. Full of love, creativity, and compassion, in oneness we exist and have our being. Being one and the same, when one of us heals themselves, when one of us overcomes the illusion, when one of us awakens, it creates a powerful shift in all our consciousnesses. By being unified in one mind, we all awaken, we all overcome the illusion, and we all heal at a subconscious level.

One of my teachers once said that when one person becomes prosperous, they become a powerful force in the world, because they are stepping into and embodying the nature of the Divine. My teacher didn't talk about material prosperity only, but all prosperity—in spirit, in mind, in body, and the world.

This is why it is important to understand that when you are thinking about something, everybody knows about it at a subconscious level. Whatever energy you dwell in, everybody feels it. Your energy is your greatest responsibility. When you create within yourself, or let other things create within you low-vibrating energy, you are dragging the entire human consciousness to that level. Remember, whenever you feel despair, it is not only you feeling it, we all feel it. When you nurture yourself and take care of your energy to vibrate higher, you are actually taking care of all humanity.

There is no greater act of love towards others than loving yourself, nurturing yourself, stepping into your Divine nature, and blossoming into your True Self. Your elevated energy lifts and nurtures others because your consciousness is part of everyone's consciousness.

This is why you can never hurt others and not hurt yourself. The law of karma is interpreted from the perspective of a mind believing in separation, but it's really the proof of our oneness and our unity in spirit, in consciousness and in God. What you do onto others, you do onto yourself, because there is no place in consciousness where you begin and the other ends. All is One.

Choosing to embody the Divinity within you will ultimately solve all problems. When you embody the God within you, you choose to embody a very high-frequency energy. In consciousness, this frequency heals, resolves, and nurtures all because it affects all. Vibrating high will change your life. When you vibrate at the frequency of Love, at the frequency of God, you become a powerful creator. And because the positive thoughts and beliefs that you nurture in your mind in order to vibrate higher every day wash over your consciousness frequency, you will be creating with the Powerful Energy that you embody. Ultimately your positive beliefs and thoughts become your reality. This is why understanding oneness is so important. You are never alone in creating your life and the lives of others; you are the only one that decides to believe your True Self or your ego every day. No matter the physical proof of what your ego is trying to convince you of, remember, the physical originates in the spiritual realm. So, you need to take care of the spiritual reality of yourself first and the physical will manifest accordingly.

Studying, meditating, praying, sitting in silence, and paying attention to the present moment will all lead to stepping into the Truth of who you are, finding the God within you, and becoming acquainted with the Oneness of all that exists.

INTUITIVE THINKING

In his book *5 Steps to Freedom*, John Waterhouse says: "Divine Presence lives inherently within us which means we always know what to do. We have an innate wisdom within us which guides us through life." The reason that we are confused, choose fear, or feel we are so out of the equation is that we live in our ego identity. The ego convinces us that we are so separate from the Universe that we might make a mistake and get slammed or kicked out of it. What an insanity to think about Life this way when we are actually the center and the whole Universe lives within us! The Persian poet Rumi said: "You are not a drop in the ocean, you are the entire ocean in a drop." Knowing that the mind of God thinks through you, through your mind, how can we doubt ourselves? The problem is we think we are these separate, petty little humans roaming through life trying to not get hurt.

One of the greatest lessons I had about the nature of my intuition and inner guidance was at a crucial time in my life. I was going through a very difficult time in my marriage, and I went to see the priest at the church I was attending on Sundays for advice. During our meeting, I brought up a desire I had for quite some time about my prayer practice. I told the pastor that I feel like I need to have a more structured prayer practice and that I could not continue to just pray whenever I need help and while washing the dishes. I told him that I had no idea how to sit quietly or what to do during prayer besides asking God for favors, but I felt this pulling desire that I needed to do something more. His answer surprised and elevated me at the same time.

He told me I was being blessed and that God was calling me to sit in His presence. My first thought was questioning if this thinking and desiring was not my own creation or doing; I wondered if these thoughts about my prayer practice are actually coming from a different source. Then I realized God thinks my thoughts and gives me my desires! Since that moment I started to become more aware of Who is leading in my thoughts and my desires.

Intuitive thinking is not some sort of special feeling or thoughts you have. It is really hard for something that feels so natural to feel different and special, but intuitive thinking does have certain feeling signs. You usually feel peaceful, at ease, elevated, expanded, and liberated. If you are used to dis-ease, then of course intuition will feel different because you have been so out of alignment with yourself that these feeling of ease might feel special. But as you grow more used to intuitive thinking, you'll realize how natural it truly is.

The more present we are in the moment, the more accessible intuitive thinking becomes. When we dwell in the past or the future, the thoughts we think are usually not in alignment with our True Nature. It is important to know that to be more of your Divine Self, you need to pay more attention to the present moment.

Ernest Holmes said that your mind is part of the Mind of God, that it is impossible to think outside of it. You are breathing into the Divinity of your Source; your thoughts, your desires, and your feelings are sourced in God. You cannot exist outside of your Divine Nature. The ego only tricks us into believing we are separate, but even in our insanity, we are still existing in the love, joy, freedom and nature of the

Most High. Love is who we are and any time our thoughts, feelings, and desires do not align with it, we feel discord.

So remember, your intuition is not just that hint you get from time to time. Your intuition is those thoughts that cause you to expand, to feel free, and to elevate to a higher vibrating energy. Intuitive thinking is not only for some people, it's for everyone. Intuitive thinking is the thinking of our True Self. When we decide to step into this, we are automatically connected to intuition and we start to think intuitively. When there is no illusion, intuition does not feel special and different, it is something natural that comes easily.

DIVINE ENERGY

I've been on a journey of self-transformation and spiritual awakening for a decade now. When I look back, what I see is me trying to let go of, heal from, and fix something in my life. But even now, I become so preoccupied with things of this world that I totally lose myself in the illusions of it. My ego tries to attach itself to a lot of things, which happens to every one of us all the time.

For example, when I finished the previous chapter and saw that I am starting this last chapter, I felt a little nostalgic that I am finishing the book. Inside my mind, I was saying, "Oh, it is almost done. I don't want to be done with it because I felt so good writing it."

But the Divine Presence replied, "Why are you attaching yourself to the book? Don't you trust that greater things are following it?" I felt a reassurance and let go of my nostalgia. I have to remind myself every day that no matter what I become busy with, there is only one place I have to be: right here and right now.

Now I know and understand that every single moment is meant to get me to only one place within myself: the Love Field. The Love Field is in this present moment, where the energy of God can awaken us, transform us, and heal our consciousness. All the transformation takes place in order for us to arrive at this place in our consciousness where we fully embody the energy of God. There is really nothing else that needs to get accomplished for us to be happy, to feel whole, and to feel alive. When we express the nature of God within us, we automatically feel incredibly good, joyful, serene, and peaceful.

There will be many times in your life when your ego will try incredibly hard to lead you astray with its illusions and directions, and you might even confuse it with your Divine Source sometimes. But remember, anxiety, depression, despair, and any negative resistance you have is a sign that you have fallen into the perception of the illusionary vision of your ego. In moments of total uncertainty, you need to know that there is Someone who knows everything, and that Someone loves you greatly and is for you, with you, and within you every step of the way.

We don't need to live our lives in fear and anxiety. We can rest and let go of all that is not ours to hold and carry. Little children know this very well; they never try to take their parent's responsibilities. It is the same with us too. There is a Creator that brought us and filled us with life, and we need to trust that this Creator knows what to do and is in charge.

169

We know very well that it is not us who decided to be filled with life. So why worry? There is no need to try and control life when we know very well deep within us that we can only participate in creation by embodying the Divine Energy within us. By stepping into the Love Field, we embody this energy, feeling love, joy, peace, freedom, and certainty that this Energy within us is powerful, eternal, and nurturing. God, Love, is in all and everything.